Don't Look Behind You

Following Ghost Roads Into the Unknown
True Stories from Toad Road and Other Strange Places

written and illustrated by

Timothy Renner

Photographs by the author except where noted.

DON'T LOOK BEHIND YOU

ISBN-10: 1729629253
ISBN-13: 978-1729629253

DEDICATION

To the mad ones who wander from the paths.

CONTENTS

ACKNOWLEDGEMENTS

Edited by Catherine Diehl.

Joshua Cutchin provided the foreword, proofreading, and valuable advice.

Afterword by Clinton Granberry.

I

A NOTE ON SPELLING AND GRAMMAR

Regarding "bigfoot" - since this is a name of a group of entities, not one individual, I do not capitalize bigfoot. I also use "bigfoot" as both the singular and plural (like "deer"). Some other authors have attempted to standardize the grammar for bigfoot, insisting that the plural is variously "bigfeet" or "bigfoots", however to my ears both of these terms hold more problems than simply using the term bigfoot universally as the singular and plural. Until the Oxford English Dictionary weighs in on the subject, I will stand on "bigfoot". Pun intended.

A NOTE ON WITNESSES IN THIS VOLUME

It can be very difficult to get witnesses of the paranormal to tell their stories. Fear of ridicule, the desire for privacy, and any number of personal reasons may account for this reluctance to come forward. I consider it of utmost importance to protect the identity of any witnesses who are willing to share their stories with me. Therefore, in most cases, I have used only first names in this volume. In other cases I have changed the names of witnesses to protect their identities.

FOREWORD
by Joshua Cutchin

I almost dismissed Timothy Renner.

The moment is etched in my mind. I was running early morning errands, and some nonsense—a watch repair, perhaps—had drawn me to the local department store, a place I rarely visit. Eager to escape the reality of fighting through throngs of holiday shoppers, I jammed in my earbuds and queued up the latest episode of *Where Did the Road Go?*

A Pennsylvania legend tripper. Collector of quaint local folklore. Some Renner guy. My finger hovered over the delete prompt.

The unexplained is like an addiction. You get hooked on the cheap, easy stuff—usually ghost stories or urban legends—and slowly, your tolerance builds. You need more and more fanciful stories, events with more profound implications, paradigm-altering theories. You know, sex-crazed space Sasquatch from Zubenelgenubi.

The idea of listening to someone digging up old stories about their town—*"Oh, is there a Cry Baby Bridge? What about a Goatman? You mean this old factory is haunted by a Lady in White? How* novel*"*—did not appeal to me. Small stakes, likely largely fabricated tales from small town Americana.

Listening to that would be like handing an alcoholic a bottle of mouthwash. At the same time, this paranormal podcast junkie needed his fix. I pressed play.

Imagine my surprise when, after ten minutes, I realized this wasn't paranormal mouthwash… *this was handcrafted, single barrel, 100 proof paranormal bourbon.*

Several years later, I am still struck by my arrogance. Timothy Renner singlehandedly revitalized my interest in urban legends and local folklore. This wasn't some naïve ghost tour guide, wearing a black tracksuit, parading around his hometown, separating tourists from their vacation dollars—this was a focused, dedicated, *honest-to-God* investigator making concerted efforts to parse fact from fiction, separating myth from reality—all while embracing the fact that, *yes, weird things actually happen.* Renner is the gold standard for what every locally-based researcher should be: well-versed in the history of his area; eager to dispel fallacies, yet equally quick to acknowledge genuine anomalies; open-minded; willing to sacrifice hours of time for on-site research; all while keeping a finger on the pulse of trends in the paranormal communities at large.

I specify "communities," because Renner is also something of a polymath. Too many researchers are drawn to the Siren's song of one particular field and spend their entire time researching only one subject: *solely* UFOs, *solely* cryptozoology, *solely* ghosts. Renner has managed to resist that, realizing that some sort of connective tissue links these topics together.

What is behind this thing, The Other, as Renner has taken to calling it? He isn't sure, and it is for that precise reason he has remained open, to "sit with the messiness of the mystery," as our Dear Saint Terence of McKenna once quoth. To Renner, the mysteries he investigates may find their answers in any of the above fields. They may be real, may be fiction, or may, in some unknowable manner, be both. He embraces the ambiguity and presents his findings with a measured, mature honesty sorely lacking in this field.

With *Don't Look Behind You*, Renner continues his tradition of what he does best: intensely focused examination on what is, for lack of a better term, a "window area," a locale where weirdness seems more *normal* and *natural* than *para*normal or *super*natural. Without hyperbole, Renner may literally be one of the best in the

IV

country at the highly specialized technique of taking one single, small stretch of earth—in this case, Toad Road and the soon-to-be-infamous Site Seven—and wringing out of it a staggering amount of legends, history, eyewitness accounts, and firsthand testimony. *Something* strange is happening in his little corner of Pennsylvania, and Renner is on the front lines.

I mean that quite literally. Unlike many researchers, Renner possesses willingness to put his money where his mouth is… or rather, his boots where his books are. A large portion of *Don't Look Behind You* (as well as his excellent podcast, *Strange Familiars*) is dedicated to his own personal experiences on site, in the field. It's harrowing stuff.

Keeping with the rest of his work, Renner presents these as agnostically and honestly as he is able. The overall message Renner conveys—argued in the work of other researchers much less convincingly and articulately—is that the human experience, especially the *personal* experience, is wholly inseparable from The Other.

That's it. My story of how Timothy Renner made me rethink my own town's legends and stories.

By the end of this book, you'll have one, too.

Introduction: We're All Mad Here

In my first book, *Beyond the Seventh Gate*, I borrowed a term from other researchers to describe that strange place where the paranormal seems to dwell: the Goblin Universe. It's a good term as it suggests a place of weirdness, a place where monsters are real, that somehow intersects with the mundane world in times and places of significance.

I have, over time, started to use the Goblin Universe less and less as a term to help describe the paranormal. The Goblin Universe sounds, to my ears, like a defined area. It sounds in some ways like a known. As I dig into cryptid and paranormal research more and more, I feel like we are dealing with very few knowns. What we are dealing with is the unknown.

For this reason I have borrowed a term often used by host Seriah Azkath and my fellow guests on the paranormal radio show, Where Did the Road Go?: "The Other". I am not sure if the term originated with anyone from WDTRG, or, if indeed, they borrowed it, in turn, from another source. I have to admit that I feel as if I am the least well-read of Seriah's regular guests - who each seem to be able to quote various paranormal, UFO, and ghost data with encyclopedic recall. So it may be that the term comes from a very well-known source in the paranormal field and I have either forgotten its origins or haven't read the book from which it originated.

In any case, I feel The Other is a more suitable term for describing the paranormal; the Fortean; the weird; the high strangeness which seems to surround the entire field of study. Ghosts, cryptids, UFOs, and other mystery lights not only all seem to issue from some kind of eerie Other place, but they also seem to defy our logic and expectations. They act in ways that are, quite literally, alien to us. The baffling synchronicities that surround the field seem to suggest a kind of Other consciousness manipulating our perceptions and expectations in unexpected and surprising ways.

It has been noted by various researchers that when people experience The Other, they are often in liminal spaces. In the case of Toad Road, it is a quite literal, physical, liminal space. It is a closed road, forsaken. A place of urban legend and forgotten folklore - a place that lies between - with residences on one end and the Codorus Furnace and some very old ruins on the other end.

Sometimes, however, the liminal space is the witness himself. Investigation often reveals that witnesses are in some sort of change-of-life at the time they encounter The Other. Often people have paranormal experiences while traveling, moving house, or after a major life event (for instance, I had a series of strange experiences about the time I moved back to my parents' farm after college).

To investigate The Other is to enter into liminal spaces intentionally. This applies more to the field investigator than those who simply do book research - as we are placing our bodies and minds into this liminality - but it can, and often does apply, even to the researchers who never get out into the field. The weirdness will come to you - sometimes in very subtle ways. My beloved wife, ever the skeptic (and I am glad for it) is fond of telling me: "You're all crazy." By which she means all of us in the paranormal, witness and investigator alike.

She isn't wrong. To try to engage The Other is like playing chess blindfolded in four dimensions on an ever-changing fractal chessboard with an opponent who has 16 queens and a different set of rules. I know how crazy some of these things sound. Disappearing houses. Toad-men. Fish-men. Mothman. Dogmen. These things can't be *real*, can they?

Even my own experiences, related herein reek of "crazy"... though I think they are somewhat more mundane than Fish-men or flying humanoids. Trust me, at the time I experienced these things - even in the moment - I was thinking, "This is madness." When does coincidence become synchronicity? My belief is that it is when a coincidence has meaning or personal significance. Finding a skull on one bigfoot investigation is a coincidence. Finding skulls on 70% of my bigfoot investigations becomes something to note, especially given the additional factors related to my story - which I disclose later in this volume. Still, to enter into this game of weird math is to entertain madness. When you begin to assign meaning to coincidences, you are playing in insanity's toy box.

On the other hand, to ignore these coincidences - to deny their strangeness and discount their meaning in order to appear less crazy - is, in my mind, a losing battle. To whom would I be trying to appear sane? Mainstream science? Skeptics?

So maybe we *are* all crazy, witness and investigator alike. If we are all crazy, we are not all liars. If we are crazy, it is because our minds or our eyes were touched by The Other - and, perhaps, forever changed. This is the madness of the liminal. This is the madness of artists and shamans. This is the madness of cunning men and wise women. This is a madness of folklore and legend - and as much as the modern world tried to shut it out with electric lights and reason - it will not be forgotten. People from all walks of life are seeing these things, and have been seeing the same things - or things very much like them - for as long as we have been keeping record. This is a madness that has been with the human race forever.

It is, I believe, a *necessary* madness. Humans have built great cities where bright streetlights and open-all-night businesses ensure that it never *really* gets dark. We have built strong homes to keep us safe, fed by electricity to keep the lights on - and to keep our minds on the television or the internet. Safe in the electric glow of our monitors, we have forgotten folklore. We have forgotten the faeries and giants and monsters who have always lurked in the dark woods beside us - and we have made the tragic mistake of confusing folklore with fiction.

There is a saying amongst traditional folksingers: A bad song doesn't get to become traditional. I believe this applies to folklore as well. Though the stories may be swollen with symbolism or exaggeration at times, they have persisted for a reason. This reason, I believe, is that the stories transmit knowledge. Sometimes it is very practical knowledge - about what plants are poisonous, for instance, and what plants may be useful for healing the sick. Sometimes these stories pass knowledge of The Other. Dig into the folklore - be it Old World tales of the fae folk or First Nations' legends - and you will be surprised how much the creatures of yore seem to look and behave like the cryptid creatures people are encountering today.

It may be that big, hairy wild men, UFOs, and human-animal hybrid creatures are all dredged from our collective unconscious. Jungian archetypes or tulpas conjured from the darkest areas of our minds. Does this make these things any less *real*? They are leaving more than questions in their wake. They are leaving footprints, hair, and scat behind. Sometimes they leave physical wounds upon their victims; in other cases, mental wounds in the form of a lifetime of nightmares.

Whatever these things are - actual physical creatures or some kind of phantom forms used by The Other for reasons beyond our ken - they do seem to be able to manipulate things in our reality. They leave physical evidence behind. They touch things. They move things.

And, yet, we never seem to capture a clear photo - much less capture a body of these weird beings, alive or dead. I believe we must move beyond this way of thinking. "Extraordinary claims require extraordinary evidence" - this is a favorite saying of the skeptic. The skeptics' definition of "extraordinary evidence" seems to be quite…well, ordinary. They want a body or a fossil record and nothing else will do. How terribly mundane. How absolutely ordinary.

I am long beyond trying to prove anything to the skeptic or mainstream scientist. I will leave that to the self-proclaimed Cryptozoologists. If they roll a body of a bigfoot or other cryptid creature into a lab one day, they will have made my job much easier. I will be able to move from writing about The Other and all its attendant weirdness to instead writing about rare, but, otherwise natural animals. So much synchronicity will become, then, mere coincidence. However, mainstream science wants nothing to do with Mothman, Fish-men, or even bigfoot. We, who pursue such things, are not welcome at their table - unless it is a "dogfight" (aka an ugly date contest) - and we are present only for them to prove how smart and science-y they are while making fun of us.

I think we have to start looking at cryptids from different angles.

The UFO community, by and large, has shifted from thinking of UFOs as nuts-and-bolts craft and started to explore alternate possibilities. Ideas of consciousness, co-creation between the phenomenon and the witness, and the possibility of inter-dimensional travels (versus interstellar) are just some of the theories currently being considered.

We need this kind of thinking in regard to cryptids. Leave the door open to finding a relict hominid or rare primate (in the case of bigfoot) - but let us look at things through other lenses as well. Let us look for the truly *extraordinary* evidence.

This is going to require engaging with The Other. This is going to require adding the experiences of the investigator to that of the witness - for by merely investigating these things, you have entered into that game of blindfolded chess. The eye of The Other is like Sauron from Tolkien's *Lord of the Rings*. Entering into paranormal investigation is like slipping on the One Ring. The great eye sees. You will attract the attention of The Other.

The question is, will The Other get your attention…and how? Will you ignore the synchronicities springing up in your life; the weirdness that seems to follow you home from these haunted spaces? Will you ignore the EVPs and other unexplained voices you catch on tape? Will you ignore the mystery lights seen around bigfoot because will-o-the-wisps and UFOs "have nothing to do" with undiscovered primates? Will you ignore all the common factors that these various areas of the paranormal share - hauntings, UFOs, and cryptids - because it's just too *crazy* to be researching all of these phenomena together?

I am done pretending it's not crazy. My wife is right. This is madness. What follows are stories of madness: of hairy giants, UFOs, half-man, half-animal things, red-eyed flying humanoids, synchronicity, and half-remembered tales from decades past. This book asks you to believe in monsters. That's crazy, right? Monsters aren't *real.* … right?

They are as real as the footprints they leave behind. They are as real as the warble of fear in a witness's voice as he relives what he encountered. They are as real as the known animals we keep in cages in our zoos… but they will not be caged. The Other plays the game by its own rules. We can participate in the game, but we will probably never win. That shouldn't keep us from trying. If answers are not forthcoming, there is plenty of mystery and wonder to go around. That's the kind of crazy I can get behind.

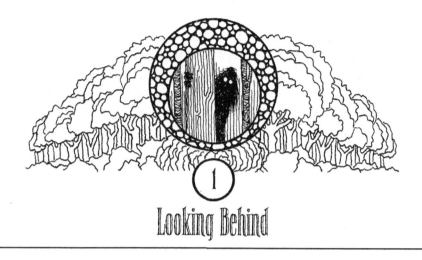

Looking Behind

This volume complements my first book, *Beyond the Seventh Gate*. That volume goes to great lengths to dispel some outrageous urban legends and outright fictions which have been penned about Toad Road. As a matter of review for those who read the first book, and to lay groundwork for those who have not, I will briefly discuss some of the more popular urban legends and historical inaccuracies associated with Toad Road - as well as some of my findings which dispute those legends. To explore these legends and my research in greater detail, please see *Beyond the Seventh Gate*.

Toad Road is a section of road, long closed since Hurricane Agnes washed it out in 1972, which runs along the Codorus Creek in Hellam Township, York County, Pennsylvania. It was originally a longer stretch of road - up until the early 1900s it extended from Pleasureville east and then north on what is now Druck Valley Road, on to what is now Trout Run Road where it continued north until it met and ran parallel to the Codorus Creek. Toad Road's original destination was Codorus Furnace, an early iron forge situated in the Hellam hills which produced, among other wares, cannons and cannonballs for the Continental Army during the Revolutionary War and the War of 1812. Toad Road would have been used to carry supplies to and from Codorus Furnace.

Codorus Creek, which was navigable water at this time, would have also been used to transport materials from points south to Codorus Furnace and / or the Susquehanna River. The Codorus flows in a northward direction from points south, including York City. The first iron steamboat ever built was carried by the Codorus, which joins the Susquehanna River just north of Codorus Furnace. Parts of what became Toad Road were likely once the towpath used to aid barges through the creek. In fact, this is perhaps a derivation of "Toad Road" - as watercraft were once towed along the way - it was perhaps called the "Tow Road", or perhaps people remembered it as the road from which boats were towed. It isn't a far leap, pun intended, from "tow" or "towed" to "toad".

For generations, legends of strange activity have been told about the area of Toad Road and Codorus Furnace.

The most popular legend associated with Toad Road came in later years - the story of the so-called Seven Gates of Hell. This story is told with numerous variations, but it usually boils down to the idea that along Toad Road, there was either an insane asylum or a kind of mad doctor who kept insane patients at his home. As the tale goes, the asylum or the doctor's home caught fire, and those residents who did not die in the flames, wandered through the nearby woods and were killed by local people, who were, for some reason, afraid of the escapees. Seven gates were allegedly erected to keep people away from the burned ruins. In the years since, a legend arose that as one passed through each of the seven gates, things would get spookier, stranger, and more frightening. It is said that no one has ever returned from the seventh gate. The area is purportedly populated by various ghosts of the victims of the legendary asylum fire. This insane asylum / mad doctor legend seems to be, mostly, a product of the post-internet age, as well as several books on local legends and ghost stories which promoted it as *the* story of Toad Road.

A view of Toad Road.

The problem is, history doesn't bear out any of the details of this story.

The closed section of Toad Road - that which is considered the focal point of supernatural activity - has never had a structure larger than a small hunting cabin built along its way. In fact, there has never been a building used as a dedicated mental hospital in York County. Nor were there ever seven gates erected along Toad Road. There is, however, one gate at the south end of the road - a simple and common galvanized gate the likes of which can be seen on farms all over America. This one gate, emblazoned with "No Trespassing" signs and sealing off the now-private land, has helped this Seven Gates of Hell legend stick to Toad Road. There was, as I will relate later, another gate of interest, known to pre-internet legend seekers - not on Toad Road, but just off of the road, leading

4

to the residence of a falsely maligned doctor.

Unfortunately for his legacy, this doctor, H.P. Belknap, lived along the last section of Trout Run Road heading north, at the southern end of Toad Road. It is a matter of some debate, but I believe this section of Trout Run Road was part of Toad Road during the time Dr. Belknap was alive. In some of the legends, and in at least one of the ghost story books which features the Toad Road legend, Dr. Belknap is named "The Mad Doctor". Again, history simply doesn't bear this out, as Dr. Belknap, a heart specialist, did not treat patients for mental illness. Moreover, Dr. Harold P. Belknap, a veteran of both World Wars, was a noted member of the York community, providing free medical care at the Society for Protection of Children and Aged Persons Homes. There is absolutely no evidence that Dr. Belknap was involved in any nefarious activities - nor did his home burn down.

Some have said that Dr. Belknap was not overly fond of trespassers - threatening them in various ways and keeping his property well-posted with warnings against trespassing. This may well have been the case. Who could have blamed him? He had moved to what he presumably hoped would be a quiet country residence with his second wife, only to find it the destination of legend trippers and rowdy young folks looking for a place to "party". If true, this only places Dr. Belknap among countless other land owners concerned for their property (and potentially even for the well being of the trespassers). It does not make him a "mad doctor". Angry, perhaps, but not mad.

As to the Seven Gates of Hell legend - this recurs elsewhere around the country, the state, and even elsewhere in York County. The Seven Gates of Hell have also been located by various legends in "Hex Hollow" in southern York County as well as in Prospect Hill Cemetery in York City. In fact, as a collector of local legend and folklore, I had heard the tale of the Seven Gates of Hell attributed to these other locations long before its association with Toad Road.

The first story I heard about Toad Road came from my wife

Codorus Creek as seen from Toad Road.

in the early-to-mid 1990s when she recounted the short warning she heard regarding Toad Road while at day camp in the area in the early 1980s: "Don't look behind you on Toad Road." This eerie phrase stuck with me for many years.

For all of my debunking of outrageous legends associated with Toad Road, I have collected many stories of paranormal activity in the area. If witnesses are to be believed, very strange things have happened and continue to happen in the area of Toad Road. If you look at these reports, however, very few of them involve ghosts. Even among the stories which do seem to report ghosts, the spectres appear to have little association with asylum escapees or victims of tragic fires.

For the most part, what people report in the area is more associated with cryptid activity. Bigfoot, dogmen, and other strange entities; the mysterious black dogs which seem to pop up around so many locales where paranormal activity is reported; weird humanoids; screams from the woods; unseen bipedal things pacing people from the brush, just out of sight; glowing red eyes staring from the darkness; orbs and other mystery lights; and shadowy things peeking from behind trees. All of these things are more often associated with cryptids than ghosts.

Looking back to that first fragment I heard about Toad Road - "Don't look behind you" - I found reference in Pennsylvania folklore to a warning the First Nations people of Pennsylvania gave to the Europeans when they first arrived in these lands. The newcomers were told to beware of something called The Hidebehind. This creature was known to follow travelers through Penn's Woods, peeking from the trees and snatching unsuspecting victims. It was said that when traveling through the forests only the bravest should be the last in line - for it was only the bravest who could be relied upon to *never look behind*. To look behind and see The Hidebehind stalking you through the woods spelled certain doom. From its behavior, The Hidebehind would seem to be another name for bigfoot creatures. Bigfoot witnesses have reported seeing the creatures peeking from behind trees. Bigfoot are often said to pace witnesses - or to follow them - through the woods. Researchers like David Paulides, who writes of mysterious disappearances of people in the wilderness, have noted that, in many cases, the missing persons were the last in line of their party - and while there is no clear proof that bigfoot is the culprit, there are some who suggest bigfoot creatures may be responsible for snatching these people. If they are not the same thing, The Hidebehind and bigfoot seem to share a lot of common ground - most notably the woods of Pennsylvania.

It has been my experience that where there is cryptid activity, there is often other paranormal activity as well. As I reported in *Beyond the Seventh Gate*, the ultimate destination of Toad Road, Codorus Furnace, has several ghost stories tied to the forge and surrounding grounds - so ghosts cannot be entirely taken out of the weird paranormal melting pot that is Toad Road. Still, most of the strange activity reported in the area seems to match up with reported cryptid behavior.

As seems to be the case with each book I write, upon publishing, I receive more information which I would have liked to include in the book. It has been no different with *Beyond the Seventh Gate*. Since its publication, readers or listeners to my podcast have come forward with new information, new experiences, and new sightings of the strange. To these, I have added my own experiences, as well as additional discoveries, and assembled this volume - perhaps the first of a series, if I receive more tales of the area. In some of the stories that follow, I have changed the names of the witnesses as they wished to remain anonymous, but I have done my best to otherwise relate the stories as they were told to me.

As I mention whenever I address Toad Road: To all legend seekers - this area is private property, posted and patrolled. Please respect local residents' right to privacy, peace and quiet. Besides this, there are parts of the area which are quite dangerous - even removing possible paranormal threats from the equation, the landscape itself is unforgiving. The Codorus Creek is polluted and unpredictable. The route is unclear and unmarked. There is no parking in the area - and parking along the road is likely to get your car towed (and tip off anyone, including the police that someone is trespassing in the area). Drive by and look if you must, but please stay off of private lands.

Haines Lodge - in disrepair, before Dr.Belknap assumed ownership.

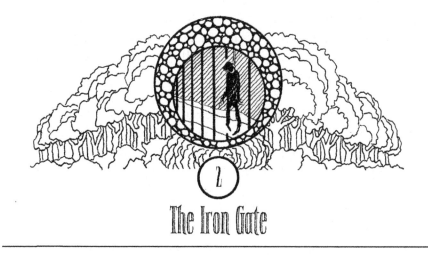

The Iron Gate

"There *WAS* a gate!"

Several people who visited the area from the 1950s through the 1970s told me this after they read my book or heard me speak. I had been very dismissive of the idea of gates, having debunked the Seven Gates of Hell legend, but perhaps I had been *too* dismissive. The large gate at the end of Dr. Belknap's drive was a place frequented by legend trippers in the 1950s-1970s. They recounted tales of just one gate, however, not seven - and no burning asylums or portals to hell. It was just someplace they went to experience the weird.

In *Beyond the Seventh Gate*, I point out several true stories from nearby Toad Road which share features of the Toad Road legends. For instance, there was a building which was once named the Pennsylvania Osteopathic Sanitorium in Hellam, not terribly far from Toad Road, and this building did in fact burn to the ground in 1949. It is important to note, however, that "sanitorium" in those times did not exclusively mean "insane asylum" but was a term applied to any institution intended for medical rest. The building in question was a retirement home, not an insane asylum. The cause of the fire was a faulty chimney. No one died in the fire or on the surrounding grounds in the wake of the fire. However, the fact that this building did burn somewhat close to Toad Road has, I believe, helped the legend of burning asylums and so forth "stick" to Toad Road. The fact that the gate to Dr. Belknap's property was also a destination for legend trippers has made it easier for the fabricated "Seven Gates" legend to "stick" as well - after all, there *was* a gate which people remember.

The first to tell me about the old iron gate was Georgeanne, a very nice woman who grew up in the area. Georgeanne now works in the medical field, but in 1978, as a teenager, she and a friend made the hike from Codorus Furnace south on Toad Road all the way to the old iron gate, just off of Trout Run Road. In 1978 there were still clear remnants of the road. Today, parts of Toad Road are little more than a path. It's hard to imagine cars drove the route less than 50 years ago, as in some places, it is now almost impassable by foot.

This old iron gate, huge and ornate, guarded the entrance to the home of Dr. Belknap and his second wife - a building that was at one time known as The Haines American Legion Lodge but would be renamed Harbeth by the Belknaps (more on Harbeth following). Before it was Haines American Legion Lodge, the property was known as Rocky Hollow, which is a very appropriate name for the area. If you follow Toad Road down to where it meets the Codorus, boulder fields and large rocks abound in the hollow cut through the Hellam Hills by the creek. (It is worth noting that elves and other faerie folk - which seem to me to be folkloric expressions of The Other - are sometimes said to make their homes in boulders and rock formations.)

Haines American Legion Lodge was also referred to, at various times, as Haines Hunting Lodge or simply the Legion Lodge. In one newspaper article it is reported that Dr. Belknap and his second wife would be living in "Lee Lodge" in Hellam. I am certain this was an editing mistake and the article is referring to the Legion Lodge.

In newspaper articles from the first half of the 1900s, Haines Hunting Lodge was a noted landmark on the road to Codorus Furnace, beside Codorus Creek (often called "Codorus River" in those days). While this road is unnamed in the old papers, as most rural roads were, it is Trout Run Road / Toad Road by its description and destination. After considerable searching, I was able to locate photographs of the Haines / Lee Lodge both before and after Dr. Belknap took over the property (he made considerable improvements and additions to the buildings on that site). This stone structure sat some distance from the road, but it was gone by 1978 - or at least Georgeanne didn't see it when she made her trek that summer.

I can locate no records of when, exactly, Dr. Belknap's former residence was torn down - but oddly, there is a story related later in this volume wherein the house was seen one week in 1973 and could not be found by the same person one week later. As best I can tell, the Belknaps lived at Harbeth until at least 1977. The house could have been torn down by 1978 when Georgeanne hiked there, but it should have been there in 1973. Is something strange happening with this house itself?

Nevertheless, Georgeanne reports that there was no house there when she visited the grounds. The large gate was extended with sections of wrought iron fencing on either side, but one could go around these fences and proceed beyond the gate. Georgeanne and her friend slipped past the gate and fences and made their way along a wide path or driveway which curved away from Trout Run Road and into the woods. Less than ¼ of a mile back, the path came to an oval section, in the middle of which was a large, flat-topped stone Georgeanne described as altar-like. The stone was about 3 feet long and 18 inches wide. She noticed no foundation or remnants of any sort of house in the area. The altar-like stone, however, has stuck in Georgeanne's mind… as did the feelings she and her friend experienced in the area of the stone. They were "spooked" as Georgeanne said, and felt the need to beat a hasty retreat and to retrace their steps back to Codorus Furnace.

The Hanged Man

There is another story of this huge iron gate that has found my eager ears, also told by people who visited the area of Toad Road long before the internet age. More than one person has told me, a man was found hanged from that iron gate, possibly in the 1960s. It's an eerie story, and the kind that could easily be an urban legend - a fiction created to scare folks, or, like some of the other legends associated with Toad Road, a half-truth or misremembered story that got bound up in all of the other spookiness attributed to the area. The story of a man who was hanged, or hanged himself, from a large, ornate iron gate is the kind of story that gets remembered. It's the kind of story that *sticks*. It is also the kind of story that is very difficult to confirm.

Without the name of the deceased or a more specific date of the hanging, it becomes very difficult to find information. I can prove that no insane asylums ever existed in York County, I can find information on Dr. Belknap and other personalities who have been named in the Toad Road story - but half-remembered tales of hangings whispered down the lane for generations are another matter. I have searched and searched with no luck. As newsworthy as such a story seems, it's possible it didn't even make the papers at the time. It's also possible I simply haven't found the story yet.

What I can do is *ask* people. People that remember those iron gates.

Having heard this hanged man story from multiple sources previously, I asked Georgeanne if she had heard this tale. She replied that she had, long ago, but could not state if it was rumor or fact. Such is so often the case with these legends. I asked her if the gate was big enough and substantial enough to bear the weight of a hanged man. "O yeah," she replied.

An uncle of a friend had also heard the tale. He recalled, with great fondness, fishing in the Trout Run stream and visiting that area in his youth. The tale of the man hanged from the gate was the only strange or scary story he could recall about Toad Road.

Be it true story or urban legend, it is difficult not to wonder at the symbolism of a man hanged on the iron gate. The hanged man calls to mind, of course, gallows folklore. Pieces of the gallows themselves were thought to have healing properties against fevers, and a splinter from the gallows in the mouth was thought to cure toothaches. The rope of the hanged man worn around the neck could cure headaches or provide good luck. Even the body parts of the hanged man were imbued with power - the hand of the hanged corpse was thought to cure a multitude of ailments such as swelling, tumors, cysts, and goiter.

However, there is one bit of gallows folklore that fits in the Toad Road puzzle especially well. One of the places black dogs were said to haunt, according to English folklore, were gallows. Black dogs are a very interesting element of the supernatural, often reported around graveyards and in areas where other paranormal activity is reported. Sometimes, these black dogs are reported as giant canines with red glowing eyes; sometimes as shadowy, ethereal manifestations; and sometimes they seem to take the form of what would be considered a regular dog, were it not being seen in such a strange place or situation. The United Kingdom has perhaps the best documented history of black dog sightings and folklore, but black dogs have been reported for centuries across Europe and in the New World - including Toad Road.

The image of the hanged man extends easily to Odin. Odin hanged from a tree, self-sacrificed to gain wisdom, was known as the Lord of the Hanged and the Lord of Ghosts. The hanged man of the tarot recalls Odin's sacrifice. The story of a man hanged from this iron gate is charged with potent symbolism. The gate, which would open to many mysteries, was positioned near to the closed section of Toad Road - what most people now consider to be the "start" of Toad Road. The gate, which keeps so many secrets behind it, mounted with a hanged man, and perhaps watched over by the single eye of the Lord of the Hanged himself.

I continue to search for any evidence that the hanged man story was a real person hanged from the Harbeth gate. I am doubtful, however, that I will find such evidence. Real or not, I feel it is a good bit of folklore for Toad Road. The hanged man story has time, possibility, traditional mythology and folktale behind it. As such, it is much more fitting than some fiction about mad doctors and burning insane asylums. That is the stuff of pulp horror and B-movies which detracts from the true mysteries of the area. The story of this hanged man, heavy with symbol and tradition, is much more in tune with Toad Road.

The Harbeth Mystery

In the spring of 2017, I received a call from a number I did not recognize. The number originated in Florida. The man left a voicemail for me stating that he wanted to talk to me about Toad Road. This was a message too tantalizing not to follow up.

I called the man that evening and had a very nice discussion with him about Toad Road. Though now retired and living in Florida, he had grown up in the area and remembered it very well. He said, for thrill seekers in the 1950s and 1960s, the Toad Road destination was "that big ornate iron gate." He added another detail about the gate - across the top of the gate, amongst the ornate patterns, was the word "HARBETH" forged from iron.

"What do you think Harbeth means?" he asked.

I replied that I had no clue. I had never heard of it before. I suggested, perhaps it was the maker of the gate, but added I couldn't be sure.

"Well, you're not much of a detective. I thought you were a good researcher," the man replied. This ribbing, good-natured as it was, stirred something within me.

Whatever my faults I am a fairly relentless researcher. I had done the footwork *and* the bookwork (and newspaper-work, and microfilm-work, and genealogical-work) to get as much of the true history of Toad Road as I could into *Beyond the Seventh Gate*, whereas others had simply published rumors and fiction. I put boots on the ground as well as nose in the books. I was proud of my research.

Swallowing my pride, I simply stated that I would look into it to see what I could find. Before we hung up, the man passed an odd bit of trivia my way. He said there was a farm in Hellam, near to Toad Road, named "Avalon". This Avalon, however, was not named for the mythical island of Arthurian legend but for two people named "Ava" and "Lon", respectively. I felt this bit of information came out of left field as it had little to do with much else of which we talked. However, in the notes I was making as I talked to this man, I scratched "Avalon = Ava + Lon" even as I was thinking it was a note I would likely never need.

All night I wracked my brain. I had a new clue, "Harbeth", but what could it mean? Why was it on that gate? I did internet searches, with no local results. There is a Harbeth Drive in Pittsburgh, but that is on the far side of the state. Did the gate's makers once have a business there perhaps? Search after search revealed nothing of use.

Something about the word had a familiarity to me, but I could not figure it out. I pestered my poor wife all night with question after question. Had she ever heard of a family in the area - or a business - by the name of Harbeth? Did she think it could be the maker of the gates? Hours of research on Toad Road brought nothing of use.

Then I stared at my notes from the earlier telephone conversation. "Avalon = Ava + Lon". It hit me like a bolt of lightning.

Doctor Belknap's first name was Harold. His second wife's name was Lisbeth.

Harbeth = Harold + Lisbeth.

This also confirmed to me that the mysterious iron gate was indeed the gate to the Belknap home. While it had long been part of legend that the iron gate was Dr. Belknap's, I never fully trusted the information until that moment.

I was eager to call my informant and let him know I solved the puzzle, but it was quite late. I called the man first thing in the morning and told him my revelation.

He said, "Oh, you *are* a good detective after all!" I was vindicated.

The conversation continued, however, and the man said, "All of that supernatural mumbo-jumbo associated with the area - you don't *believe* that, do you?" I stated my belief that witnesses have little to gain from reporting such events, and tend to face ridicule and derision when they do come forward, so I believe people are seeing and experiencing something.

The man replied that he thought it was all nonsense. However, without a hint of irony in his voice, he proceeded to tell me a story about a ghost cat which came into his bedroom one night. He felt the cat's weight as it leapt onto his bed. He pet the cat and asked how it got in the house and, as with so many of these strange encounters that happen as people wake in the middle of the night, he simply went back to sleep, rather than pursue the matter of an unknown cat in his house. In the morning he searched everywhere but found neither the feline nor any open doors or windows where the cat could have gained entrance or made a subsequent escape. He was about to write the incident off as a strange dream when his wife asked him why he was petting a cat in bed the night before, and where the animal was currently located.

With my research skills vindicated, and a neat story of a spectral feline as a bonus, I was satisfied. I then asked him if he had ever heard of a man being hanged from the iron gate. He replied that he had not. I asked if the gate was substantial enough that a man could have hanged himself from its bars. He said that it was. I also asked him if he ever remembered seeing statues of toads or toad-like gargoyles on the gates or surrounding property (it is sometimes reported that Toad Road gained its name due to these toad statues that were on or around this gate). He replied that he never saw any such thing in the area. We said a pleasant goodbye, and I hung up the phone.

It was some days later when I thought back to that strange detail in my notes: "Avalon = Ava + Lon". It seemed irrelevant to the rest of our conversation at the time. I began to believe that the man knew exactly what "Harbeth" was and that he was testing me to see if I could figure it out. For what reason though?

I looked back to my notes to find his name / number. I had not written them down. I went to my voicemail to listen to his initial message. I had deleted it. I could find no call to or from Florida in the call history on my phone. I couldn't even call him back to ask him if he knew all along what "Harbeth" meant. Those phone conversations, and this man whose name I have forgotten, have become just another mystery among so many associated with Toad Road.

Iron

Part of research, especially when dealing with things weird and paranormal, is connecting the dots. Many revelations have come to me when I was able to connect A to B and B to C. The flip side to this equation is that sometimes one starts to make connections where there is only coincidence. The danger then is moving from discovery into a type of "conspiracy theory" thinking.

However, I would be remiss if I did not point out that this big ornate gate, with the word "Harbeth" worked into its design at the top, was made of iron. Iron ore, worked by the hands of man, became "cold iron" and was known to ward off trolls, faeries, goblins, witches and all manner of supernatural pests and fiends. This folklore seems to have transcended cultures - "cold iron" being the solution for supernatural woes in many places worldwide. The best-known example is probably the horseshoe. This popular symbol of good luck came from the fact that they were blacksmith forged - cold iron - and therefore a tool for keeping bad spirits away.

As I spent some wordage discussing iron and the supernatural in my chapter on Codorus Furnace in *Beyond the Seventh Gate*, I will leave off there, so I do not repeat myself too much in this companion volume. However, I'm quite certain that there is enough folklore and legend regarding iron as it relates to the supernatural that an entire book on the subject could be filled with ease.

Let us note, however, that on Trout Run Road - at the south end of Toad Road, which most people consider to be the starting point of Toad Road - there stood a gate made of iron. On the northern end of Toad Road stands Codorus Furnace, an iron forge. Iron, it seems, figures into this road from start to finish. Iron was probably even the prime cause for Toad Road's beginning, as the route was likely cut to serve Codorus Furnace in the earliest days of York County industry. Iron seems to be forged to the bones of Toad Road.

Something Unseen

One night in the late 1970s, three teenagers made their way to Toad Road for a night of hopeful thrills. They got more than they bargained for. Behind the wheel of a 1968 Plymouth Super Bee, the driver wound through the dark back roads of the Hellam Hills until they came to the infamous iron gate.

The driver backed the vehicle up to the gates and cut the engine. The three occupants waited with anticipation in the darkness. Were they expecting the spectre of a hanged man? Ghostly voices? Perhaps they were only seeking the unspecific thrill that comes from being in haunted places, especially at night.

After a time, they felt the car move.

Something pushed down on the back and let up, the shocks springing the rear end of the vehicle back to its resting height. Then it happened again, this time with more force. And again. And again.

Someone - or some *thing* - with either great weight, great strength, or both was rocking the car up and down. It was as if the back bumper was being stood on - or jumped on - repeatedly.

The driver checked his mirrors. The passengers looked out of the rear window. No one saw a thing in the darkness. No one got out of the car to check. Having had enough thrills for the evening, they started their car and drove hurriedly away from Toad Road.

As with so many of the strange occurrences on Toad Road, this event was blamed on ghosts by the occupants of that Plymouth. Perhaps it was some sort of phantom spirit rocking the car - as the culprit was unseen, who can say? However, this behavior of hitting or otherwise messing about with people's vehicles has been reported many times by bigfoot witnesses.

Another story, very similar to this one, came to me from a local reader of my first book. The witness, we will call him Joe, reported to me that he went to the area very near to this iron gate as a young adult in the 1970s. He was with his girlfriend, and, just like the trio in the Plymouth above, they went to an area near the iron gate, where Joe pulled his car to the roadside and cut the engine. They had heard legends about unnamed spooky things that haunt Toad Road.

They were parked there for some time, when they heard something hit the trunk of their car with a loud thump. Joe checked his mirrors, and saw nothing. He looked out of the windows in every direction. It was too dark to make out much. He couldn't see who or what had hit the trunk of his car. Joe's girlfriend was silent, but wide-eyed with fear.

Her silence turned to screaming when they felt the back end of their car lift off of the ground as if it had been very suddenly jacked up for a tire change. The rear end of the vehicle was held in the air for about 8-10 seconds then dropped violently to the ground. They jerked in their seats as the car creaked and moaned under its own weight. Joe wasted no time in starting the vehicle and speeding away, his girlfriend crying in the passenger seat.

The above two stories are very similar. The first was reported to me by a friend of the trio. The second by Joe himself. These witnesses did not know each other yet their stories are almost identical. Something unseen, yet very strong was rocking and lifting up vehicles. Automobiles in the 1960s and 1970s, in general, were not the relatively lightweight amalgamations of sheet metal and fiberglass of today, but very heavy vehicles. Lifting the rear end would require incredible strength.

It is possible, however unlikely, that a human could have been rocking the Plymouth in the first story and, somehow, remained unseen. This would require a person skilled enough to remain hidden, or quick enough to push the car down, however it was accomplished, and get away before being seen. A person who was willing to wait in the shadows on this rural road in the 1970s just in case someone might show up so they could scare them. A person brave enough to risk being caught by the occupants of the car and facing whatever form their wrath might take. Still, even with all of those mitigating factors it *could* have been a human. Personally, given the history of Toad Road and the cryptid activity reported in the area, I don't think it was a person, but as I said, it is a possibility.

When we get to Joe's story, if we are to imagine it is a human, we must now add to this quick and stealthy person the attribute of incredible strength. As unlikely as it was to imagine a human as the culprit of the rocking Plymouth, it becomes impossible to imagine a person was responsible for lifting the rear end of Joe's car, while somehow remaining unseen.

It may be a leap to offer bigfoot as a possible solution to these mysteries, but given other solutions seem to require people with superhuman abilities, I don't feel like it's a claim which is particularly more outrageous. The creatures are said to be incredibly fast, incredibly stealthy, and almost inconceivably strong. Bigfoot are, in terms of their reported physical abilities, quite literally superhuman.

A 100 pound chimpanzee can dead lift as much as 600

pounds. A male silverback gorilla may be able to lift as much as 1800 pounds. An eight foot sasquatch, it is thought, could lift well over a ton above its head - and, this is if we are talking about a natural creature which obeys known laws of physics, eliminating any kind of preternatural powers or abilities bigfoot may have which we just don't understand. Something with that kind of power could easily lift up the rear end of an automobile.

There is one more Toad Road story I have collected which has very similar elements to the stories above but ends quite differently. It is this story, more than anything else, which makes me believe bigfoot creatures may have been the unseen culprits harassing the motorists in this chapter.

Monsters Are Real

I felt one of my most interesting finds in researching *Beyond the Seventh Gate* was a short newspaper article about Michael, a man attacked near Toad Road in 1973 by what he described as a "green haired monster". The brief story noted Michael was admitted to York Hospital for treatment and that the police found no monster.

Michael was difficult to track down and even more difficult to get to speak about his encounter. It took me months to draw the details out. Even at that, I do not have the full timeline of the encounter as Michael didn't like talking about what he witnessed and would often change the subject. More than 40 years after his encounter, he was still experiencing horrible nightmares. These bad dreams got worse when he talked to me about what he experienced. Sometimes for weeks after he talked to me, he would be plagued by these nightmares. I am not a mental health professional, but in my layman's view, it seems likely that Michael is suffering from a form of Post-Traumatic Stress Disorder (PTSD) all these many years after his encounter. So, when Michael stopped returning my calls, I did not press the issue. I wanted to document his story, not torture the man.

Michael lived just across the Susquehanna River from Hellam, in Lancaster County. Legends travel easily across rivers, and York County's Toad Road, with its mysterious iron gate, was well known to him and his friends. In the early summer of 1973, 18-year-old Michael and a friend decided to find that iron gate.

As an aside, there is some debate as to whether Toad Road was ever officially called Toad Road. Many say it was just a nickname. I believe Hellam Borough's website even states there never was a Toad Road. Others, myself included, seem to remember seeing a Toad Road road sign at what is now the last section of Trout Run Road before the corner where the closed and gated section of Toad Road is today. This was before the internet infamy and Seven Gates of Hell stories became so popular. Michael told me he remembered seeing a Toad Road sign as well.

Back to the early summer of 1973.

Michael and his friend did, indeed, find the iron gate. Some distance behind the gate, he remembers seeing a large stone house. Just beyond the gate, Michael and his friend saw pear trees, heavy with fruit. They slipped behind the iron fences to get a better view. The fruit was ripe - rather early for pears, Michael noted, as they usually ripen in late summer in Pennsylvania. As if lured by the serpent in Eden, they tasted this forbidden fruit. Michael said that to this very day, he has never eaten a better-tasting pear. They picked a bunch of the fruit and took it home. Michael's mother liked the pears so much that she asked Michael to go back for more.

A week later, Michael and his friend returned to the area, but he said there were no pear trees visible, nor any sign that they had ever existed. Stranger still, he said there was no trace of the stone house. Only the gate remained.

I have tried to reason how this may have happened. Trees get cut down, for various reasons... but for a house to just disappear in a week would be very unusual. Not impossible, but highly unlikely. I have record of Dr. Belknap and wife living along what is now Trout

Run Road until at least 1977. Could they have torn down the stone house and built another structure in its place? Did Michael just happen to visit the property a second time between one structure being demolished and another being built? What are the chances?

I had thought for a time that with 40+ years in the past, Michael was perhaps remembering a *much* later visit - perhaps around the time of Georgeanne's hike in the late 1970s. Further discussions, however, lead to the revelation that Michael has never been back to Toad Road since his third and last visit, in the late autumn of 1973.

Disappearing pear trees and houses. It's the kind of weird detail that is tempting to leave out of the story because it seems *too* fantastic. However, as I have examined strange phenomena, I have found that weird details seem to surround these mysteries. I have been admonished by some bigfoot researchers for talking and writing about all of the *other* oddities which often surround sightings - UFOs, orbs, and other mystery lights; other, stranger cryptids; ghosts; black dogs; and more. I have been told: "They will never take us seriously if you keep talking about all of that other stuff in association with bigfoot". I do not know exactly who "they" are - presumably mainstream science and/or media? My answer is that I think it is irresponsible *not* to discuss everything the witness reports - or even if a second witness reports a UFO in the same general area and around the same general time as a separate bigfoot sighting - these events should be noted. Who is to say if they are connected or not until we know more about both UFOs and bigfoot? Besides this, "they" already do not take the subject seriously. We are, after all, talking about an eight foot tall ape-man wandering around in the woods of North America.

Michael relayed one more thing about that second visit to Toad Road. As he and his friend roamed around the area of the gate, mystified by the missing trees, his friend started getting very uncomfortable. Echoing Georgeanne's sentiments, Michael said his friend told him he got a very bad feeling from the place and they decided to leave.

Michael would make his last visit to Toad Road late one night in early December, 1973. Seeking a spooky thrill, he was drawn back to the area of the iron gate. He pulled his car off to the side of the road and cut the engine. He sat there in the dark for some time, noting an eerie silence hanging over the area.

After a time, Michael decided to move on. He turned his key in the ignition, but the car would not start. Before cell phones, on a dark and lonely rural road, a driver had few choices in this situation. You could get out and try to figure out what is wrong with the vehicle. You could start walking. Or, you could wait and try to start the car again or hope someone willing to help happened along. Michael chose to wait.

Some time passed in darkness and silence. Michael was almost resigned to sleep in his car, until he heard something. It sounded like something brushed up against his vehicle, but he couldn't see a thing. The silence returned for a while and then he heard it again. This pattern continued for what seemed like hours. Something would come out of the silent night, brush against Michael's car, then creep away without being seen.

Eventually Michael decided he couldn't stay in the vehicle any longer. It was between 4:00 and 5:00 AM when he decided to make his way on foot and seek help. The pre-dawn morning was dark and chilly. I looked up the moon phases and the weather for the night - there was a sliver of a moon - not yet the first quarter, with partly cloudy skies. Michael wasn't getting much light from the moon.

Whether to stay warm, to put distance between himself and whatever was brushing up against his car, or to try to more quickly seek out help, Michael began to run. He ran through the darkness seeking a house with a light on perhaps, or a passing vehicle. He found neither.

Michael ran until he ran into *something*. Michael didn't have too many words for what it was, really. He said "I don't know what it was." It was big - larger than any man he had ever seen. It was upright - standing on two legs. And it was covered in hair. He said it was a "monster."

This thing, whatever it was, proceeded to attack Michael. It scratched his face and beat him to the ground. This is the hardest part for Michael to discuss, understandably, and the timeline here gets uncertain. I do not know who found Michael - or even if Michael knows how he was found - but he ended up in York Hospital. His injuries kept him in the hospital for a week. He was partially paralyzed with a serious head injury. When he returned to school, Michael had to be helped from class to class.

The police, when they talked to Michael, suggested first that he had encountered a man "dressed in skins". When Michael refused to agree that's what he ran into - saying it was just too big - the police then told him he had run into a cow. Michael lived on a farm. He knew what cows were. This was no cow.

The police retrieved Michael's vehicle on the day of the incident. They found the back door of the car hanging wide open. Someone or *something* with hands had opened the door. The only thing missing was a large knife with a red handle that had been on the back seat. The car started with no difficulty, and the police were able to drive it away from the scene.

Michael is not a "bigfoot guy". He has no particular interest in the subject of bigfoot. At the point I talked to him, he had never even considered that he could have run into a bigfoot creature. He only knew it as a monster. When I asked him, "Do you think you could have run into a bigfoot that night?", I was met with several seconds of silence and then a quiet reply: "You know, I never thought about that. Maybe that is what it was."

With so many modern reports of bigfoot creatures hitting, pushing, or brushing up against cars - and perhaps, more disturbingly, with other reports of vehicles not starting in the vicinity of bigfoot creatures, only to start without issue at a later time -

Michael's encounter has become a sort of bigfoot checklist.

Bigfoot attacks are rare, but not as rare as some bigfoot researchers would have you believe. The idea that they are gentle forest giants just doesn't always seem to be the case. Bigfoot creatures seem to have a very short temper and a kind of "culture of revenge". If they are shot at or attacked in any way - they have been known to fight back - sometimes even following people to their homes, only to exact revenge at a later date or harass the residents by slapping the walls, climbing on roofs, and making a general nuisance of themselves.

I have collected another story of another man literally running into a bigfoot creature at night in the 1970s. This story comes from Westminster, Maryland. The creature, known as the Hook Road Werewolf, was seen by many, running through the local orchards at night. It was called a "werewolf" not because it had a wolf's head - it wasn't a dogman creature. It was a bigfoot by description, but in the 1970s, and sometimes even today, some people hold the idea that "Bigfoot" lives in the Northwest, and anything in the eastern states which meets that description must be something else. This is one reason we get localized names for bigfoot like "Gum Devil", "The Hidebehind", and the like. In this case it was the Hook Road Werewolf.

As the story goes, told to me by a friend of the injured, a young man was running through the woods in the area of Hook Road one night and just happened to run square into the creature. It broke his arm and threw him to the ground. The Hook Road storyteller had not heard of Michael's account (nor Michael of his), but the stories are incredibly similar.

Whatever Michael ran into, it made a lasting impact on his life. Nightmares still plague him over 40 years later. It is understandable, for in December of 1973, he found out that monsters are real.

Orbs, Howls, and Eerie Music

Christine called me to talk about a different but equally strange subject to Toad Road. She has been experiencing paranormal activity of various sorts for some time. This is not unusual, as I find these events tend to cluster both around certain locations and certain people. Some people seem to be paranormal "magnets" (or perhaps "lightning rods" would be a better metaphor). As she told me her stories of shadow people, visions, orbs, and UFOs, she casually mentioned that it all seemed to start on Trout Run Road.

That detail certainly caught my attention.

It turns out that Christine's family lived on the southern end of Trout Run Road for some time. Her family owned a farm where Christine ran an animal rescue and kept various animals in the barn. I asked her if she had any experiences in the area of Toad Road. Indeed, she had.

The first thing Christine mentioned is the thing I hear reported more than anything else from Toad Road, as far as unusual experiences: screams and yells from the woods. She heard them frequently coming from the wooded area behind the barn on her family's property, but also from the south - from the area of the closed section of Toad Road. She also reported what sounded like rock clacking and wood knocks.

Christine was also witness, on multiple occasions, to an orange orb. It appeared to be about the size of a basketball and would travel across the fields just above the ground, or move just above the treetops. On one occasion she placed her dog in the car and followed the light. It moved over the treetops. Christine was able to follow the orb as she drove along Lower Glades Road, west of Trout Run Road, until it finally moved over the Springettsbury Wastewater Treatment plant and then disappeared over the trees beyond.

On another occasion Christine followed the orange orb on foot. It was moving over the fields, parallel to Trout Run Road. After some distance, the orb seemed to notice her. It got brighter and turned its direction toward Christine. She turned around and ran to her automobile, feeling it was a better idea to chase strange lights from the relative safety of a car. However, when she looked for the orb again, it had disappeared.

Christine would often be out at nighttime tending to animals in the barn. One night she was standing beneath a fluorescent dusk-to-dawn light, mounted to the garage, which helped her see her way to and from the barn in the dark. She could hear it buzzing above her. Then, from the direction of Toad Road, she heard what she described as a very loud explosion - at which point the light above her head went out. She noted that only this light went out - she could see that other lights inside the residence were still lit.

Following the explosion sound, Christine heard what she at first thought were dogs barking. This would not have been terribly strange as such a loud sound would no doubt wake and alarm any local pets. However, the sound grew louder and louder, and she soon realized this was not the sound of dogs barking, but something with much greater volume and lung capacity. She described it as a bark, howl, and scream somehow combined into one loud cry. This frightening howl sounded two or three more times. In its wake, Christine was greeted with the distant sounds of some strange music.

Christine hesitated before telling me that last detail. Perhaps she was thinking it was just *too* weird. She didn't know I had heard similar things before, even in York County.

On the same night as the explosion and howls, Christine also saw the orange orb again.

On another night, Christine was driving on Lower Glades Road when she saw something which appeared to be a wide chevron shape, adorned with blue lights, flying low in the sky. She noted that it seemed to be smaller than an airplane - perhaps 12-feet wide. She couldn't see if there was something like a craft to which the lights were affixed or if they were in some other way linked and flying in formation. She followed this UFO as it turned to follow Trout Run Road north, toward Toad Road. Echoing the orb she followed, this UFO whatever it was - seemed to get brighter as Christine followed it. This frightened her, so she pulled her car off to the side of the road as the UFO continued on its way. Suddenly a car came speeding from the north, blowing its horn wildly as it went. As they passed, Christine noted the occupants seemed to be frightened.

As we talked, I brought up Mike Clelland's amazing book, *The Messengers*, which deals with owl symbolism and synchronicity, particularly in relation to the UFO and abductee phenomena. Owls seem to be tied into paranormal phenomena in very strange ways - it would take a book to explain it all. (That book is *The Messengers*, by the way.) However, even a passing exploration of the topic will reveal that owls are often seen before and after UFO sightings as well as in conjunction with other paranormal events. Even bigfoot have an owl connection with many, many witnesses reporting that the creatures mimic owl sounds - some have reported hearing something like "an 800 pound owl" hooting in the night. So, I reacted with great interest, but without much surprise, when Christine mentioned that she had seen and heard many owls around the farm on Trout Run Road during the time of her experiences.

Christine, like Michael, wasn't really a bigfoot person. At least she wasn't as obsessive about the topic as I am. She never considered the screams and howls could have been issued from a bigfoot creature. She certainly didn't know there was any connection between orbs, UFOs, and bigfoot.

The connections are unclear, but well-established. I have written multiple times that if you show me a bigfoot sighting in Pennsylvania, there is a good chance I will be able to find a UFO sighting around the same place and time. This doesn't apply to every sighting, nor even *most* sightings, but it seems to apply to enough sightings that it must be noted. I always clarify that I do not think bigfoot is flying around in UFOs or being transported by alien beings to our planet. The truth is, I don't know why these things are seen at the same times and places, but for whatever reason, they *are*. As I have mentioned previously, I think it is irresponsible as a researcher or documenter of the strange to not at least note these things.

Even the strange music has been noted in cases involving both bigfoot and orbs. This is one of the rarest sonic anomalies associated with either bigfoot or orbs, but it has been noted in cases involving both. I have collected another story of this, also from York County. After I published *Beyond the Seventh Gate*, in which I discuss Rehmeyer's Hollow (aka Hex Hollow) along with Toad Road, as a place where multiple paranormal phenomena are reported, a good friend and sometime bandmate of mine, Zach Nace, told me the following story:

One night in 2006 or 2007 he was driving the back roads through Hex Hollow with a friend. They were bored and simply driving around the lonesome roads. They stopped the car to sit and talk. It was a warm night, so their windows were down. Behind them they noticed orbs hovering in the darkness. The strange lights seemed to be coming toward them. In silence they sat, almost hypnotized, and they heard an eerie, ethereal, almost angelic sounding music drifting upon the night air. Eventually, the driver started the car and they drove away from the scene. They drove in silence for some time until the felt they were a safe distance away from the orbs and strange music, when they stopped and compared notes. They both agreed on what was seen and heard.

I was in some disbelief that Zach had not shared this story with me before I finished writing my first book, but it is a good example of how things sometimes go with witnesses to the paranormal. As I write about strange phenomena, it is in my mind almost daily. For other folks, even people who have witnessed these phenomena, sometimes it just isn't a major part of their lives. Some witnesses just don't think about their experiences too often. Others just don't *want* to think about their experiences. In Zach's case, it just didn't occur to him to tell me the story until one night when we were sitting around and the subject of Hex Hollow happened to come up in conversation. I was disappointed it didn't make it into *Beyond the Seventh Gate*, but I'm happy to be able to share it here at last.

Since Christine lived so close to Toad Road, and since she was around my age, I asked her some questions about the area. I asked her what she remembered about the locality of the iron gate. She told me she remembered the gate - that it was huge - and she remembered the stone house - but perhaps most interesting to me, she remembered an orchard of sorts. There were pear trees there, just as Michael said.

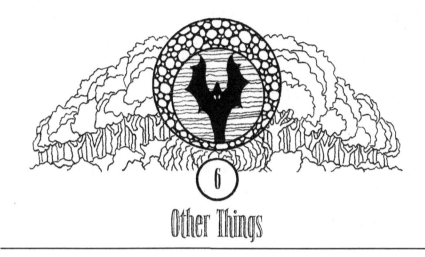

Other Things

The focus of the stories presented thus far has been on the southern end of Toad Road - where the Harbeth gate stood. Indeed, this area has been the focus of most people visiting the area - in the past, due to that iron gate; and, in more recent times due to the Seven Gates of Hell legend. It is only natural that most encounters will occur in this area as it is where people were going.

However, we must not forget the northern end of Toad Road and its original destination: Codorus Furnace. The great forge stands as a monument to the earliest industry of York County. A huge tower thrust up from the Hellam Hills, it once spewed smoke and ash and flame as molten iron poured from its base, only to be worked into various items - not least of which were the implements of war: cannons, cannonballs, and grapeshot. Weapons are perhaps the *coldest* iron of all.

Now Codorus Furnace stands silent - a ghost of brick and stone which haunts the landscape along Codorus Creek. Though the forge has been repaired and rebuilt several times in the past, it retains the look of something lost to another age. People who pass the forge daily, often don't know what it is or what its purpose once was. No wonder so many ghost stories are told about this place.

Stan Gordon has been collecting stories of strange encounters in the Keystone State since the 1950s. While his main focus has been the western region of the state, Stan's considerable experience in this field, as well as the respect he has earned for his thorough and level-headed research, means he often receives stories of encounters from across Pennsylvania and even reports from other states.

Stan received a report from the Codorus Furnace area which he forwarded to Lon Strickler of the Phantoms and Monsters website, and Lon, in turn, shared it with me. There wasn't a ton of detail in the report - only that a witness reported that he had seen a dogman creature in the vicinity of the old forge in the autumn of 2015. The witness was very specific on the appearance of the creature - it looked like a huge upright-walking hyena.

Dogmen seem to be what we might have called werewolves in the past: bipedal canine creatures, with hands or hand-like claws on their forelegs / arms. It is thought that dogmen are not humans that transform into wolf-creatures, as is the case in werewolf mythology, but things which are always in their canid-humanoid form. Sightings of these creatures have been on the rise in Pennsylvania, and elsewhere in the country. While I personally believe at least some dogman sightings are misidentified bigfoot, I don't think that can account for every sighting. Some bigfoot witnesses report the creatures having baboon-like snouts or a prognathism of the jaw. So just because someone says it looks like it had a snout or a dog-face does not, to my mind, immediately suggest dogman. The tell-tale signs of a dogman seem to be doglike ears visible on top of the heads and the hocked or crooked back leg (like the back leg of a dog). In any case, the description of an upright-walking hyena seems very specific - it doesn't sound like a case of someone seeing a bigfoot and mistaking it for a dogman.

These upright hyena things seem to be some kind of variant

of the dogman creature. They have been reported elsewhere in Pennsylvania and further abroad. What they are is anyone's guess. If one were looking to reason bigfoot as natural creatures of some sort, then an undiscovered primate or relict hominid are good working theories. While I feel neither of those is a very likely answer to the bigfoot mystery, those theories remain possible, and one could see bigfoot taking a place in the natural tree of evolution et. al. It is hard to imagine where upright wolves - or even stranger, upright hyenas - would fit into natural science. Even if they did, what is an upright hyena doing in America? It's not like it was an exotic pet which escaped.

It is worth mentioning, as well, that hyenas are not even canines. Though doglike in appearance, hyenas are not just another wild dog but are, in fact, from an entirely different family of animals, taxonomically speaking. If these hyena-type dogman creatures are related to hyena in the way many cryptozoologists assume dogman creatures are related to wolves, we now have to believe in some kind of convergent evolution of upright wolves and upright hyena. This is asking a lot of even the most ready believer. It seems like dogman - whatever form it takes - must be some kind of paranormal entity.

Folklore from Africa and the Near East - those places where hyenas are native - hold tales of various sorts of were-hyenas. Some varieties were said to be hyenas which hold the ability to transform into a more humanlike form (as opposed to humans changing into a hyena or some sort of creature which takes a form in between human and hyena). Most relevant to the story at hand, given the multiple iron connections and the proximity of Codorus Furnace, are the Ethiopian were-hyenas, the Bouda. The legends state that these Bouda are blacksmiths - both their trade and supernatural powers being hereditary - transforming into were-hyena at night, robbing graves, and generally terrorizing the community.

When Lon first shared this bipedal hyena report with me, the date didn't really strike me. It was a few days later that I realized autumn 2015 would have been when I was deep into researching and writing *Beyond the Seventh Gate* and spring of 2016 was the first

The mystery figure I photographed on Toad Road.

time I had hiked the entirety of the closed section of Toad Road. I thought back to that hike and to the strange photo I had taken along the banks of the Trout Run stream where it crosses Toad Road.

The photo shows… something odd. It is very controversial because it is blurry and it is inconclusive. I have made sure never to claim this photo shows anything because the truth is I do not know what it shows. I can only tell you that I didn't see it when I took the photograph and when I returned to the area, I could not reproduce it. Some people have said that it looks like something "morphing" into this dimension. Many people have told me it looks dog-like. When I thought about the bipedal hyena sighting I began to wonder a bit more about this image.

Of course, it is easy for the skeptic to scoff at this photo because it is so inconclusive. It's easy to just say "that's nothing" - and I have no argument against that. I have been sent, literally, dozens if not hundreds of photos of "bigfoot" taken by witnesses and asking my opinion. Often I can't see what the witness sees in the photo - but what does that mean? Only that I can't see it. Other times I can see what they are claiming to be a bigfoot, but in almost every case, it has been blurry or otherwise indistinct. I have come to suspect that there is something about The Other that somehow doesn't photograph. It is almost like these things don't *want* to be photographed and can somehow insure that we will not get a good clear photograph. With all of the game cameras deployed everywhere across the country (including multiple bigfoot hotspots), why is it that no clear game-cam photos of the creatures have ever surfaced? The same seems to apply to other cryptid creatures, spirits, ghosts, "aliens", etc. The Other seems to be fine with audio recordings - many compelling and interesting audio documents exist of various sounds related to these phenomena - but video seems to be out of the question. I am reminded of the story on Skinwalker Ranch, that hotbed of high strangeness in Utah, where cords to video cameras were cut by something unseen. There was another camera trained on these cameras, and when the footage was played back during the time that the cameras went offline, the tape showed nothing.

So, when I look at the photo I took, and I see that it is inconclusive part of me thinks: *of course it's inconclusive!* The Patterson-Gimlin film, arguably the best footage of a bigfoot ever taken, is inconclusive. I happen to think it shows a real creature, and a lot of people, both expert and layman, agree with me - but a lot of other people, expert and layman alike, disagree. And my blurry photo is so much less that the Patterson-Gimlin film. On the other hand, just because it's inconclusive doesn't mean I think it shows something paranormal. It just means it's another question mark along the way.

The hyena-thing isn't the only canid creature reported around Toad Road. In *Beyond the Seventh Gate* I noted a sighting of "dog heads too high in the trees" by someone who visited Toad Road. I mentioned in the text that perhaps dogman was an explanation for this but the report of this large upright hyena gives that idea a bit more gravitas. As mentioned previously, black dogs have also been reported on Toad Road.

A were-hyena, or whatever it was, is a very weird thing indeed. Weirder still are reports of winged or flying humanoids like the Mothman of West Virginia or the more recent Chicago Phantom flap where multiple sightings of what appeared to be a bat-winged humanoid were reported throughout the Chicago area. (As of this writing, sightings of the Chicago Phantom are still being reported.)

Lon Strickler was contacted by a witness who saw a winged humanoid creature near Codorus Furnace. He reported the sighting on Phantoms and Monsters:

The witness, Sky, lived in Mount Wolf, near Codorus Furnace. Mount Wolf, though bearing a name pregnant with synchronicity given the topics at hand, is actually named for a person, not the animal. George H. Wolf was the first railroad station agent of the locale which, bearing no name previously, was named Mount Wolf - "Mount" for the elevation, and "Wolf" after George. It is, nonetheless, worth noting the proximity of a place named Mount Wolf to Toad Road.

Sometime around 2010, Sky's mother called her outside to listen to a strange sound. They were used to the sounds of foxes and other natural wildlife, but something about this cry, which they described as "a sad lonely wailing" seemed to be different from anything else they had heard. The crying wail faded in and out and eventually seemed to drift away.

A short time after this, Sky and her mother were driving at night on Codorus Furnace Road, just past Jerusalem School Road, when they stopped the car to look for deer in the fields. Something caught their attention in the rear window of the car. They both looked back to see a tall, black figure stand up behind them and spread winglike appendages from its back. Her mother quickly sped away from the scene without saying a word.

Later, mother and daughter compared notes and agreed on what they observed: a 9-10 foot tall entity which appeared to be winged. Sky would refer to this sighting as her "Mothman experience". They returned to the area in daylight to see if there could have been a tree or something they had mistaken for the creature, but there was nothing but fields.

In *Beyond the Seventh Gate*, I cover the multiple sightings of a Mothman-like creature Lon Strickler named "The Conewago Phantom" and other locals have dubbed "Old Red Eye". Lon documented multiple sightings of this entity spanning many years - all of which were along the Conewago Creek, near New Oxford, PA. Interestingly, the Conewago Creek meets the Susquehanna River just north of Mount Wolf.

I stumbled upon an interesting bit of history, relative to the area which calls to mind the Mothman of West Virginia. A newspaper report from *The Hazleton Sentinel* on February 14, 1889 reads:

Blown to Pieces.

York, PA, Feb. 14 — A terrific explosion occurred at Johnson's Dynamite Factory, situated at Mount Wolf, this county. John Harline, an employee, aged 33, of this city, was literally blown to pieces and the factory was totally demolished. He leaves a widow and three children. It is supposed that Harline went into the nitro-glycerine magazine and in turning on a water spigot, which was frozen, the friction therefrom caused the explosion. His body was thrown over the top of a tree seventy-five feet from the factory. No one else was injured.

A search for more information on this factory led me to the following article from the *York Daily*, published on February 14, 1914:

25 Years Ago:

```
Johnson Dynamite Works at Trout
Run, near Mount Wolf, was blown up
by    an    explosion    of    nitro-
glycerine, resulting in the death
of John Harline, of York.
```

Another article I found, listed the location of the dynamite works about a mile from Mount Wolf, near Trout Run. While I have yet to find out exactly where this factory was, it was certainly in the general area of Toad Road. This adds another building destroyed by fire in the area, along with another tragic death. Some have noted that Mothman - and these other winged things, if there is more than one - seem to be drawn to areas where tragedy occurred - and sometimes where tragedy is about to occur.

Stranger than this, the area most associated with Mothman in West Virginia was known as the "TNT Area". This location, outside of Point Pleasant, West Virginia was an abandoned World War II munitions manufacturing and storage facility. Tall, winged humanoid creatures seen near former explosive manufacturing plants in Point Pleasant, West Virginia and York County's Toad Road. If it is a coincidence, it is a very weird coincidence.

The Johnson Dynamite Works is an obscure and forgotten piece of York County history. I could find no information whatsoever on the factory at the York County Historical Society or the York County Archives. I have never heard any local historians make mention of Johnson Dynamite Works. I had neither heard of nor read of the place before stumbling onto the newspaper articles above. Other than the explosion in 1889, which made its way into several papers, there are only a couple passing mentions of the factory in local newspapers. It is highly unlikely Sky or her mother knew anything about the Johnson Dynamite Works when they saw the Mothman creature.

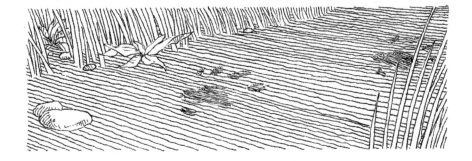

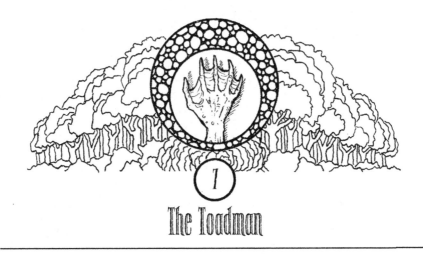

The Toadman

Cryptids are very strange creatures. Things like bigfoot seem plausible, if unlikely (I say this as a believer, by the way), because things somewhat like bigfoot exist (humans, gorillas) and previously existed (various other extinct hominids). Grey "aliens" are basically human-shaped and upright - and fit one concept of what we believe an alien race may look like - or perhaps the shape into which future humans will evolve. Don't get me wrong, greys and bigfoot *are* bizarre - but the rest of the cryptid family just seems to get stranger and stranger.

Dogman. Goatman - a hoofed, goat-headed upright creature. Rakes - hairless and impossibly skinny humanoid things. Mothman and other winged humanoids. Chupacabra. Lizard-men. The Jersey Devil. The list of cryptids goes on and on, and the further down the list you read, the weirder and seemingly more impossible the creatures become. These cryptids seem to be, in many cases, *chimeras* - combinations of two or more different animals - or of animals with humans. Though most of the creatures have some forebears in folklore and mythology, mainstream science seems to prohibit these things from existing. You simply cannot breed a

49

human with a goat and get a goatman.

Yet, people do report these cryptid creatures, and seemingly with greater frequency every year - though this may, in fact, be due to the internet making it easier for people to tell their stories and file reports.

One of the stranger cryptid creatures reported in the United States is the Loveland Frogman - or Frog*men* to be precise. At about 3:30 am one night in May of 1955, an unnamed businessman was witness to three creatures near Loveland, Ohio. Variations of the story place the creatures alongside the road, under a bridge, or on a bridge - but the descriptions of the cryptids are consistent. Reportedly, they were 3-4 feet tall, naked, hairless, bipedal, and covered with leathery, wrinkled skin. The creatures were said to resemble upright-walking frogs. One of the creatures held a metal object the witness described as a wand which emitted a series of sparks and flashes when the frogman raised it above its head.

Other reports of frogmen around Loveland have been filed over the years, most recently in 2016 when a couple reported seeing an extremely large frog which proceeded to walk on two legs. They filmed the creature, but as tends to be the case with these things, the results are blurry and, once again, inconclusive. The footage does show something with large glowing eyes which seems to have shoulders and arms, whatever it was.

So, when I was told about the Toadman who lived in Codorus Creek, I knew there was a precedent for such things being seen elsewhere. Extremely rare, impossibly weird, however, not completely unheard of.

Barb grew up in York County and visited Toad Road many times in her teenage years, before Hurricane Agnes washed out the road. She told me several stories about her youthful visits to Toad Road. Unlike a lot of the other folks around her age who remember visiting the area in the 1970s, she had very little to say about the iron gate at the south end. Barb's stories involved being on the dark part of Toad Road, by the Codorus, under the trees - down in the rocky hollow. "Do you know that area", she asked me, "where it gets *really* creepy?"

(Indeed, I do.)

Barb started by relaying tales which were on the mundane side of things, as far as Toad Road goes. She said there was a man who drove a Cadillac who would chase people on the road at night. Given all the strangeness in the area, one's mind goes to Men In Black (MIB) - those odd-mannered fellows who would show up and question, harass, or otherwise intimidate witnesses of strange phenomena (most often UFO witnesses). Often it is reported that the MIBs drive black Cadillacs. The MIB connection is, admittedly, a leap - certainly a local person, fully human and normal in every way (but for the propensity to chase people with his car) could have been behind the wheel of that Cadillac. However, the longer I pursue stories of Toad Road the *weirder* these stories seem to get. What started for me as debunking some ridiculous urban legends turned to pursuing stories of bigfoot. Soon enough tales of other, stranger things began to creep into the mix: UFOs, hyena-headed dogmen, Mothman, and, as you will read below, even Fish-men and a Toadman. It seems nothing is off the table when it comes to the weird tales being told about the area. MIBs chasing people down Toad Road? In the face of everything else being reported there, that seems almost quaint.

Barb was telling me about the car she was riding in getting stuck in a ditch when her stories turned well away from the mundane. "We were trying to get the car out in a hurry because we were worried about the Toadman," she said.

At first I just let the name float by, unquestioned. I assumed, she meant Dr. Belknap who, according to some legends, was very fond of toads. I thought perhaps she was calling Dr. Belknap "the Toadman" - and suggesting he was the man behind the wheel of the Cadillac. However, there was something in her voice when she said "Toadman" which gave me pause.

"Toadman?" I questioned. "Oh, yes, you've never heard of the Toadman?" Barb replied. I had not. She continued: "He lived down there in that creek bottom. The Toadman is the reason it's called Toad Road." I've read many reasons Toad Road may have earned that name, and made a few other guesses myself, but this is the first time I've heard it attributed to a cryptid creature. If it turned out to be true, it would be most fitting.

I asked Barb to clarify what she meant by Toadman. She told me it was what it sounded like - a creature that walked upright, was the size of a man, but had features and coloring of a toad. The Toadman, Barb said, was the greatest worry about being on Toad Road at night. "I'm not going to tell you I saw the Toadman," Barb said, "but I'm not going to tell you I *didn't* see him either."

My mind shot back to the newspaper report I found from 1973 in which Michael reported being attacked by a "green haired monster" on Trout Run Road. Then I thought of James Kibler's report of what his father saw while motorcycling on Toad Road - an unidentified humanoid creature crouched alongside the road (both of these accounts appear in *Beyond the Seventh Gate*). James has since told me the few details his father would relate about the creature was that it was green in color and frog-like, at least in the way it was crouching. These are separate witnesses, without any connections or knowledge of each other, all reporting something similar, yet very, very strange in the area of Toad Road.

They are not totally without precedent. In 1905, *The Wilkes-Barre Record* printed the following account:

Fish Walks Like a Man

Strange Animal Alarms
Residents Along Susquehanna

York City, PA, October 22 — People residing along the river midway between Cly and Goldsboro are mystified and some alarmed over the sight of a strange creature that has its abode in the Susquehanna. Thus far but two men and their wives have seen the "thing." As it was seen in broad daylight more credence is given to the story than would be if it had been seen at night, when people are more prone to see "things." The strange creature, whether fish or animal, is described as being as large as a man.

When seen it came up out of the water erect like a man and is described as looking like a man without arms.

Those persons who have seen it declare that they are not the victims of an optical illusion.

A Fishman and a Toadman may not be the same thing - but both are bipedal and presumably amphibious. Though separated by 70 years, the reports of the Fishman and the Toadman are geographically quite close. The area between Cly and Godsboro would be about eight miles north of where the Codorus Creek meets the Susquehanna River.

So many of our modern cryptids have parallels in creatures from traditional folklore. Almost every culture across the globe has a big hairy wild man, like Sasquatch. Perhaps even more widespread are the "little people", hairy dwarves reported everywhere from China to Africa; Europe to the United States; and even in the Pacific Islands. These hairy little men go by many different names but share a lot of similar behaviors and attributes, no matter the names placed on them (our own local version is the albatwitch, about which I wrote in *Beyond the Seventh Gate*).

In fact, a lot of the supposedly "mythical" creatures from folklore seem to look and act like what we call cryptids in modern culture. What we call "dogmen" today would have been werewolves in the past; not a natural animal, but a supernatural shapeshifter. Sasquatch would have been seen as wodwose, bukwas, almas, Ghillie Dhu, or any of the hundreds of other names used for what seems from their description to be something a lot like "bigfoot". Depending on the culture, these bigfoot creatures would have been seen as a faerie or spirit being and not as a rare primate.

It is worth noting that several traditional cultures *do* consider bigfoot, whatever their name is for the creatures, to be natural animals or a different type of human. I find it incredibly interesting, however, that even amongst Native American tribes, the views on the creatures are split: some consider bigfoot to be a natural creature; some call it a forest guardian; some think it is a mystical or spiritual being; some say bigfoot are just a separate tribe of hairy humans. Traditional cultures seem to be just as split in their opinions as to what bigfoot actually is as modern bigfoot researchers. If one would descend down the bigfoot rabbit hole, you would find theories to explain the creatures as diverse as undiscovered primate; relict hominid; inter-dimensional traveler; alien; ghost; Nephilim (biblical giants); and even demons. The more things change, the more they stay the same.

Besides the better-known cryptids like bigfoot and dogman, folklore holds analogues for some of our stranger cryptids as well - goatman would have been a faun to the ancient Romans and a satyr to the Greeks (see also Pan and Puck). Winged humanoids, like Mothman, are found in mythology and folklore worldwide - a short list would include the Garuda from Hindu and Buddhist mythology, the Tengu from Japan, and the various swan maidens from Celtic and Norse folklore. The Egyptians are well-known for portraying chimeric beings of various sorts - winged humans, jackal-headed gods, the sphinx and many, many more.

I was therefore excited, however not very surprised, to find the folkloric equivalent of our Toadman in various cultures across the globe. Most interesting to me was the "vodyanoi" as it is known in Russian tales. The vodyanoi is a water spirit that was said to appear like an aged man with a *face like a frog*, a *green beard*, and long hair. The vodyanoi's body was said to be *covered in muck and algae* and, sometimes, with black scales. His hands were webbed, he had a *fish's tail*, and eyes that *glowed red, like hot coals*.

The Czech equivalent of the vodyanoi, the "vodnik" or "hastrman" is somewhat more man-like in that it is said to wear clothing, albeit very strange-looking clothing. Like the vodyanoi, the vodnik were said to have webbed fingers, algae-green colored skin, and light green hair. In addition to these features, they were said to have *gills* as well. Sometimes the vodnik is depicted riding a catfish. The vodnik was said to lure children to the river's edge by placing ribbons and mirrors on the banks.

Both vodyanoi and vodnik were river spirits, feared and revered by humans. They were said to be responsible for drowning both people and animals, for stopping mill wheels, and breaking dams. They collected the souls of drowned men - the vodyanoi used them as servants; the vodnik stored them in cups with porcelain lids (apparently a status symbol amongst the vodnici, as the more soul-cups a vodnik had, the wealthier he was considered).

River spirits with frog-like faces, fish tails or gills, and green hair. How far from frogmen, or our Toadman, is the vodyanoi? Note that both the vodyanoi and vodnik were endowed each with fishlike features: a fish-tail for the vodyanoi and gills for the vodnik. Could these folkoric creatures account for our Fishman as well? So many cryptids are reported as having glowing eyes that it seems to be an almost universal feature. The frogmen from Ohio are no exception - and the vodyanoi had glowing eyes as well. Are all of these things just coincidences - or were the folktales of our ancestors simply describing the same weird things people are seeing today?

These cryptid creatures seem to defy science while confirming folklore. I realize this statement is almost koan-like in its "logic". We are talking about things which defy logic and reason. We are talking about creatures which mainstream science says simply cannot exist. But there are records, in the form of folklore, of creatures that meet these strange descriptions. Our ancestors saw them before, just as we see them today.

Folklore celebrates a vast ecosystem of strangeness - a menagerie of weird monsters woven into a world alive with spirits. We closed the books on folklore and started calling it fiction. Perhaps it's time we start looking at folklore as something that is more than just fiction - it is describing The Other. What we thought were simply "fairy tales" may instead be *tales of the faeries* - weird creatures which inhabit liminal spaces, as real or as unreal today as they were thousands of years ago. Today the cryptid witness is doubted or ridiculed - especially if they report something as "crazy" as a toadman. In another time, perhaps, the doubt and ridicule would have been awe - for the Toadman was not simply a chimera (as science would have to explain it) but a river guardian and, perhaps, an avatar of The Other.

The Shaking Tree

I met Jeff after my first appearance on the *Sasquatch Chronicles* podcast. I went on the show to talk about my book, *Beyond the Seventh Gate,* including Toad Road and the associated mysteries. Jeff is a local man with a deep interest in bigfoot. After hearing me speak about Toad Road, Jeff, along with his girlfriend Lori, started to visit the area with some frequency.

Jeff, who considers himself a bigfoot enthusiast, as opposed to a researcher, started pointing out many interesting anomalies around Toad Road - mostly in the form of tree structures. Tree structures are one of the most difficult forms of "evidence" that surround the bigfoot mystery. Ostensibly, these broken trees are created by bigfoot creatures for a purpose at which we can only guess. Most bigfoot researchers presume they are trail markers, territory markers, or some other kind of sign to other bigfoot. There is a big problem with tree structures: snow load, rot, and wind damage causes many trees to bend and break. A lot of what people believe is "evidence" may, in fact, just be nature taking its toll.

I was fooled by Mother Nature myself early in my search for bigfoot. I came upon an area of multiple tree breaks near Hex Hollow in York County. As I observed the different breaks and the directions the trees had fallen, it became clear that this was not storm damage. It seemed too many breaks in one area to just be a coincidence. I started photographing all of the breaks and looking for other evidence in the area. After multiple visits, I realized that all of the broken trees were pines and the surrounding woods was predominantly deciduous trees. What happened was the deciduous trees came in, grew tall, grabbed all the sun, and the pine trees rotted and fell at various times - in various directions. It's a perfectly natural process. However, eagerness to find bigfoot sign has led to many a misdiagnosis, and I am not immune to that fault. I was somewhat embarrassed by the fact that it took me multiple visits to sort out the cause of these breaks, but I had a good laugh at myself and moved on.

On the other hand, there are structures which seem too complex or otherwise impossibly assembled for nature's hand to have played a part. These include "teepee" structures, twists, and arches woven together in such a way that someone or some*thing* with hands had to be involved. Even in the area I described in the previous paragraph - about a year after I diagnosed it as "nothing to see here", I found an arch which was created by using a very large cut log to weigh down the top of a live tree. It was obvious this log didn't *fall up* into the tree. The tree was bent over and the log was used to weigh the top down, creating the arch. The tree was big and heavy - it wasn't a sapling - the log was heavier. Could people have done this? Yes, it's possible, but I think it would have to have been more than one person. If it was people, why would they do this?

In any case, tree structures are a perplexing and difficult piece of the bigfoot puzzle. They are, nevertheless, deeply interesting to me. Though we may not be able to say for sure the tree structures are definitely made by bigfoot, we can say, like the weird light phenomena, for whatever reason, tree structures seem to appear around areas where bigfoot is reported.

The sheer number of broken trees on Toad Road is interesting. The road itself, that part which is still potentially passable on say, an ATV or snowmobile, has a tree pushed down across the path every 30 yards or so - making it impassable. This could be weather damage but, again, there are so many reports of bigfoot creatures pushing trees across paths to impede humans (especially those driving ATVs or other vehicles), that the impressive number of trees across the path should be noted.

It was Jeff who called my attention to the great number of broken or bent trees throughout the woods surrounding Toad Road. So many of these are inconclusive, that it is hard to say much more than the quantity alone is interesting and seems to be greater than most other places in the York County woods. However, Jeff also pointed out one incredibly interesting structure to me.

I went with Jeff and Lori for a hike around Toad Road one Sunday in February 2017. On the south end of Toad Road, along the banks of the Codorus Creek, Jeff led me to a very large X formation. Two huge tree trunks - each heavier than a single man could lift - forming an X. Many bigfoot researchers consider the large X formations to be warnings to humans. A "keep out" sign of sorts. It's not impossible for trees to fall and make X's. It happens naturally - but we could find no stumps where these trunks had broken off. Much stranger than this - one of the trees which formed the X was placed with its roots pointing skyward and the top of the tree facing down into the ground. Trees usually don't fall *roots up*.

While Jeff and I pondered tree structures and discussed all things bigfoot, Lori made her way off to sit by the creek a hundred yards or so south of where we were. After a time, Lori made her way back to where Jeff and I were standing. She reported that as she was sitting by the water she heard what she described as a low "huffing" type sound come from across the creek. As Lori pointed to the general area from which she heard the sound, I noticed a large sycamore tree waving back and forth in the woods.

The sycamores around Toad Road are tall, with white tops -

and they stand out starkly against the other trees. There was no wind on this day. The air was still. No other trees were moving - but this one, large sycamore was rocking back and forth with considerable force. I could not see the base of the tree, but it was located directly where Lori heard the "huffing" sound.

I had experienced some mild strangeness on Toad Road up to this point, but nothing truly shocking. This shaking tree, however, I could not explain. Short of a team of humans with ropes attached, pulling on the tree, or a Clydesdale horse repeatedly ramming it, I could not understand what could shake the sycamore in this manner. Neither a team of humans nor a Clydesdale were in the woods across the creek - there aren't paths or pastures in that section - just thick woods - and as mentioned previously, the Codorus is, essentially, a fast-moving river in this area - it's no gently flowing creek. No one was crossing the Codorus on a cold February day just to hide and shake a tree when some other folks may or may not be watching.

I had smelled a strange bad smell hiking Toad Road one day (somewhat skunky - somewhat like rotten meat - a smell I would experience elsewhere in York County as I describe in the Appendix) - the smell was only in one specific section of the trail. Like an invisible wall of stink, you could walk through this section, smell the stench for about 5-10 feet, and then step out and smell nothing. However, you could turn around and walk right back into the "wall" and smell it again. I repeated this experiment several times - as did a friend who was hiking with me.

On another nighttime visit with two friends, two of us thought we heard bipedal steps in the creek. The third fellow along that evening wasn't sure. Of course, there was my inconclusive photo of the whatever-it-was I took on the banks of the Trout Run, which I have already discussed - as well as the tree structures I mention above. All of these things are *strange*, yes but they all seemed so ephemeral, inconclusive, and surrounded by so many "maybes". This sycamore tree, solid and real, its branches stark white in contrast to the surrounding grey February landscape, seemed like something else. Shaking there amidst all those other still trees, it seemed to be the first real, undeniable strangeness to greet me on Toad Road. Whatever was doing this - however this was happening - it was weird.

It would not be the last strangeness to greet me on Toad Road.

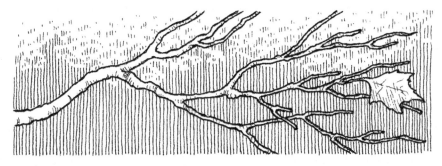

9

The Hanging Skull

In March 2017, I went for a hike on Toad Road. It's something I do with some regularity - sometimes alone - and sometimes with others. On this day I had a hiking partner, Anthony, who was responsible for many of the photographs in *Beyond the Seventh Gate.* I was excited because I had found a new way into Toad Road a few days previous - a way that lead through some of the very oldest sections of the towpath - where stonework dating back to colonial times can still be seen along the banks. Finding this section of Toad Road - a section which would have been abandoned by the 1960s if not earlier - meant I could hike the entirety of the road from north to south - something which I don't believe anyone has done in decades.

Anthony and I walked south, perhaps a mile or so, on Toad Road, before turning around and retracing our steps. On the way back out of Toad Road, in the middle of the trail, I found a perfectly clean raccoon skull. Since I was a child, I have always collected skulls I found in the woods - as long as they were clean (I am not a fan of rotting meat or gore) - and have amassed quite a collection over time. It was interesting that I had missed this skull on the way in - they are something I look for and collect, and my eyes are somewhat trained to seek out the bone-white color against the detritus of the woodland floor. However, it didn't seem like anything particularly significant. I simply thought I missed the raccoon skull on the hike south, for whatever reason, and saw it as we headed back north.

I should note here that Toad Road is not a hiking destination. People do not frequent the area. Some hunting is done on parts of Toad Road during hunting season, but otherwise it simply isn't a destination for recreation. It is private property - no one should be there without permission. On top of this, it isn't a pleasant hike - especially the north end of Toad Road. There are places where it is very difficult to follow the trail. Any trace of the road has been lost to time and overgrowth and washed away when the Codorus overflowed its banks (as it often does).

I am, however, a completist and having not hiked the *entire* road, I made plans to meet Anthony in three weeks to finish what we started. For whatever reason, when that day came, Anthony was unavailable. I decided to just do the hike alone.

Three weeks had changed the trail immensely. It was now April, and spring had well sprung. The riparian hollow that Toad Road follows had burst forth with all manner of greenery. Tangling weeds, thorns, stinging nettle, and poison ivy made what was a challenging hike rather miserable. Spring rains had left standing groundwater to soak my shoes and patches of thick, sucking mud slowed my progress greatly.

I am not usually prone to ticks. For reasons unknown to me, entire groups of people I hike with will come out of the woods, each with multiple ticks while I will not find one on my person. This day I was not so lucky. Perhaps deprived of my hiking partners, the ticks decided I was on the menu. I pulled several off of me along the way. I also had a copperhead snake come out of the high weeds and cross the path in front of me.

Ruins of a flint mill beside Toad Road.

I was there, however, and intent on pressing on with my hike.

I got to about the place on the trail where I had found the raccoon skull, when I heard something up ahead of me. I looked up to see something perhaps 50-75 yards away. It was very large and fled with incredible speed, heading southward on the trail. Whatever it was did not make another sound as it disappeared into the brush.

I have found describing what I saw to be somewhat difficult. The reason is that it was very very fast. I have said many times that the first thought that came to my head was "moose". This is not because it particularly looked like a moose. I think "moose" came into my mind due to the sheer size of the creature. I had seen a moose in Massachusetts some years prior and was shocked at the size and gait of the creature.

Moose, of course, are not in York County. Elk have not been here for two hundred years or more. Whatever I saw was simply too big to be a buck or a bear or a coyote - or anything that *should* be in the woods in York County, PA. In any case, it didn't particularly look like a moose - that was just the first thing on the checklist of "what could that be?" my mind jumped to - I think due to the size and the strangeness of movement.

What did I see? Well, it was quadrupedal - whatever it was. It was covered in hair or fur which was grey and black in color. In the brief moments I observed it, it seemed like its head was down. I saw its back for the most part. It was very tall and very broad. I can't say how tall for sure because I couldn't find the exact trees into which it disappeared to get a size measurement - it really was just a sea of bright spring green leaves, grasses, and weeds on this day - but it was *shockingly* big. I am 6 feet tall and it seemed considerably taller than me and perhaps double my width.

I can't say I saw bigfoot. The fact that it was quadrupedal does not, however, eliminate bigfoot - as many witnesses have reported that they will move from bipedal to quadrupedal locomotion - especially when they want to move quickly.

I can't say *what* I saw for sure. Someone suggested it was perhaps a bull elk that had roamed back into this area. I can't say that it wasn't - but I feel that is very unlikely. I have read several stories of ghost elk in Pennsylvania. I would sooner believe I saw a ghost elk than a natural elk - but even this I will not sign off on. It really didn't look like an elk. It didn't move like an ungulate. If pressed, I will say it appeared to be running like a gorilla or a chimpanzee.

Whatever it was, I followed it southward on Toad Road.

This was no act of bravery on my part. In fact, later that day, after the adrenaline and amazement had passed, I started shaking and had to sit down as I thought to myself: "What were you doing? You were *alone*. If that was something trying to lead you into an ambush, you took the bait."

I don't know what came over me, but without thinking, I

66

followed on. The next period of time was trancelike - and I don't remember too many details. I was focused on heading south as quickly as I could manage, given the trail conditions. I don't know how long it took me to get from the place where I observed the large creature to the place where I stopped, but I know from later hikes, I went about ½ to ¾ of a mile through very unpleasant conditions.

What finally stopped me and snapped me out of this hypnotic state, was a deer skull, perfectly clean, and impaled upon a branch at eye level, directly in the middle of the trail.

I looked around in amazement; it was not there three weeks before. I would have noticed it. Anyone would have noticed it. It was at *eye level*. In the *middle* of the trail!

If a person placed that skull on that tree, they would have had to bring a skull with them, or find a perfectly clean deer skull in the woods, hike into an area under extremely unpleasant conditions, and impale it on a branch. For what reason? To hope that one of the very few people who have permission to be in the area might just happen to find it? Sure, it's possible a person did it, but how strange a coincidence that I would find this skull on this day after seeing whatever-it-was that ran south, leading me to this skull.

I have been asked by some if I thought that this skull was a warning. For whatever reason, I didn't take it that way. Perhaps it's simply because I have collected skulls since I was a child. They don't always "read" as sinister to me. Whatever my impressions are worth, my mind shot back to that raccoon skull I found three weeks earlier. I got the feeling almost as if *something* was saying "Oh, you liked that little raccoon skull? Well, then I have something you'll *really* like." There is, of course, no proof in impressions. It was just where my mind went.

I have talked with bigfoot researchers in other areas of the country who have found bones in trees. It is their belief that these bones mark very specific areas - possibly hunting grounds. Contradictory to my impressions above, these researchers have told

The skull as I found it on Toad Road.

me that they think these bones-in-trees are in fact very much a signal of warning - or at least a sign that the area is dangerous to humans because it does mark bigfoot hunting grounds. Other researchers have reported finding skins or other animal parts hanging in trees or on shrubs in areas of suspected bigfoot activity. In York County, my fellow investigators and I have documented several cases of deer legs, seemingly torn from the deer and hanging over high tree branches. None of this is proof that bigfoot creatures hang animal parts in trees - and, it certainly isn't proof that the deer skull I found was placed there by bigfoot. It's all just another bit of strangeness to add to the pile. It's another layer of mystery inside the onion of the paranormal. Peel it away, and there's just another layer below it.

Since finding this skull, I seem to find other skulls (most often deer skulls) on a highly disproportionate number of bigfoot investigations. In fact, my skull collection has probably doubled or even tripled in size since finding the skull on Toad Road. It is quite bizarre. I have forms I fill out after each bigfoot investigation in which I participate. Most of the form is taken up by categories you might expect: witness recollections; description of the date, weather, and geography; notes on any possible evidence; distance of sighting relative to nearby creeks; etc. I have actually added a section to the form to note other, *weirder* things. One of the categories in this section is to note whether I find a skull while doing the investigation. It doesn't happen all the time - but it happens often enough that the section on the form is warranted. I have found clean skulls on almost 70% of my bigfoot investigations since finding the skull on Toad Road. None of these have been impaled on trees, but I haven't had to dig through brush to find them either. I will just look down during the course of the investigation and find a skull. It has become almost amusing now when I find these skulls. Any laughter, however, is tempered by amazement and wonder as I shake my head and try to reason out what it means and why it is happening … or if I am instead simply losing my mind in the Wonderland that is The Other - following synchronicity like Alice followed the White Rabbit - into a realm which does not obey the rules of logic and reason.

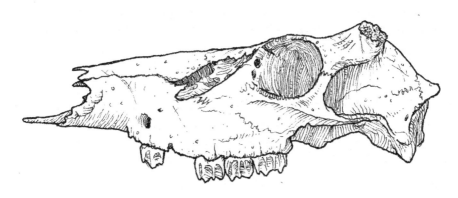

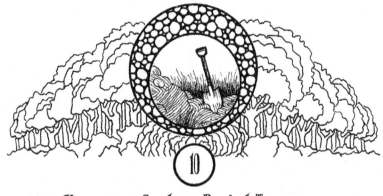

Venomous Snakes, Buried Treasure, and Half-Remembered Tales

Slithering Things

Sometimes things turn up in these liminal spaces which, while wholly natural, are frankly just out of place. I have already briefly addressed the "black dog" problem in the paranormal. While some of these canines (especially the giant ones with glowing red eyes) are no doubt of the *unexplained* variety, others are certainly just dogs - black in color, feral or pet - but wholly natural dogs nonetheless. However, when black dogs, even the mundane type, start showing up in places like Hex Hollow or Toad Road, or any of the other locations worldwide known for repeated paranormal activity, one must ask, is there more to the picture?

In other so-called "paranormal hotspots", rare animals or animals thought to be extinct have made appearances - large wolves, possibly the extinct dire wolf, have been seen in many of these locations, including Skinwalker Ranch in Utah. Things matching the description of pterosaurs have been seen as well (in York County something matching that description was seen in 2015 - see *Beyond the Seventh Gate* for more information).

Thunderbirds, huge raptors - much bigger than the largest condor known to be living today - have also been seen across the country, and, indeed, right here in Pennsylvania. One witness even reported seeing one of these thunderbirds between Pleasureville (about which we shall read more very soon) and Toad Road in 2006 - a massive bird with a 15-foot wingspan. Thunderbirds have many prehistoric precedents - including the Teratornis in North America - which could possibly account for Thunderbird sightings.

Extinct animals - or animals we thought to be extinct - are perhaps not just out of place, but also out of time - and these sightings indeed are very strange. However, as compared to something like Mothman or dogman or even bigfoot, we can at least say this much about the prehistoric creatures people are seeing: At least there is something in the fossil record that may account for the animals. In that, they are at least somewhat more natural. As yet, we have found no bones of winged humanoids, wolf-human hybrids, or even bigfoot (though some would say the Gigantopithecus may meet the criteria - just as many others would disagree).

Having noted all of the above, when I find a report of something that seems to be completely natural, but also very much out of place on Toad Road, I have to wonder if it is part of the paranormal puzzle or if it is simply what it seems to be - just something that is simply out of its normal habitat, but for wholly natural reasons.

Trout Run, the beautiful little stream that crosses Toad Road just before it meets the Codorus Creek, has some natural wonders - malachite and clear quartz crystal can found in here if one searches hard enough - but in the early 1900s George Miller, a York County zoologist and taxidermist found something that should not have been in the area.

An excerpt from a much longer article about Miller's snake collecting reads:

Of the non-venomous snakes belonging to York County, there are about all the varieties occurring in other parts of the state. Among the most common are the blowing-viper, the common black snake, the black racer, the common water-snake, the striped water-snake, two varieties of the garter or garden snake, the milk snake, and several kinds of house snakes.

Mr. Miller has in his collection what is probably the only specimen of water moccasin ever taken in York County. He killed the snake several years ago along Trout Run, while it was in the act of swallowing a large frog. The snake, which is almost three feet long, was examined recently by Prof. H. A. Surface, the state economic zoologist, who pronounced it a genuine water moccasin and a great rarity for Pennsylvania. The water moccasin is a semi-tropical snake and is rarely found north of the Potomac River. It is among the most deadly of venomous snakes.

(from *The York Daily*, April 6, 1905)

The only water moccasin ever documented in York County and it just so happens to turn up in the area of Toad Road. What are the chances? I do not ask that question sarcastically, but with genuine curiosity. What are the chances of finding a water moccasin anywhere in Pennsylvania, much less in York County, and then along the Trout Run? Whether the snake made its way here under its own power or was transported here by human agents, on purpose or by accident, it is just as strange and amazing that it ended up in the area of Toad Road. The fact that the snake was not only rare in this area, but also highly venomous, adds another twist to the mystery.

Of Buried Treasure and Its Otherworldly Guardians

As I mentioned in Chapter 9, when I investigate bigfoot encounters, I note other odd things that happen around the bigfoot phenomenon. Mystery lights of various stripes were the first anomalous things which I noticed frequently reported around bigfoot. For me personally, finding skulls has been something that happened so often I thought it wise - or at least interesting - to keep track of those investigations where I found skulls.

Another interesting detail I started to find is the idea of buried treasure of some sort being found around areas associated with paranormal activity. By "treasure" I do not mean literal chests of gold (although sometimes this is the case), but instead the idea of something valuable or secret being hidden or buried beneath the ground. Everyone has heard the tales of haunted houses being built on forgotten burial grounds and of earthbound ghosts lingering to guard their buried wealth. Somewhat less ubiquitous, but still rather common, are stories of bigfoot or other cryptid creatures occupying long abandoned mines or underground cave systems.

I was contacted by one bigfoot witness who told me a second hand story of a cave being dynamited shut in the 1950s or 1960s. The locals, he said, were afraid of what was living in the cave - though they were not specific about what this feared cave-dweller was exactly. The location, I was told, was somewhere between Glen

Rock and Railroad, Pennsylvania - in southern York County. Interestingly, one of the few other bigfoot reports I collected from the Glen Rock area dated from the 1960s - it was reported that a large "gorilla" was attacking livestock. The witnesses, at the time, said they believed the creature was living in nearby caves.

In the Delta / Peach Bottom area of York County there are a large number of bigfoot sightings dating back to the 1800s. The area is also, not surprisingly, riddled with other paranormal activity that runs the gamut from headless ghosts to UFOs. In the 1920s, Sam Glidden and his sister Ammie held seances in their Delta-area home. One of the spirits with which they believed they were in contact, told them a tale of pirates who had sailed up the Susquehanna River, landed at Peach Bottom, and buried their treasure somewhere nearby. Sam spent most of his life and all of his money looking for that buried gold, which was never unearthed.

These are just a couple local stories I have used to demonstrate this idea of buried treasure and the paranormal. It isn't difficult to find other stories from further abroad: lost gold mines; secret caves; UFOs removing some mineral or precious metal from the earth; UFOs emitted from the earth itself; the list goes on and on. Looking back to Skinwalker Ranch, reportedly the family who owned the property was warned not to dig on the land. When paranormal researchers took over the ranch, they brought in digging machinery in an effort to intentionally stir up anamolous activity. If we look to folklore, there are any number of tales of ghosts, faeries, or other monsters guarding buried treasures. The realm of the faeries itself was often said to be within the earth (often entrances were mounds or other earthworks).

I added buried treasure (in whatever form) to my list of *other* things to ask about on my paranormal investigations. Thus far I have found stories of something valuable or secret beneath the ground in the vast majority of my investigations. I am unsure exactly what this means, but it seems there is something about The Other that is connected to the earth itself.

The following article is from *The York Daily*, December 16, 1892:

Searching For Treasures

Some time ago there was found a place on Rutter's Hill along the public road leading to Pleasureville, where it is believed by some that a large amount of money is buried in the earth. About a month ago some parties from York accompanied by a country doctor went in search of this money, but failed to get it on account of the place being haunted. The doctor thought that he was able to face anything that came before him, but had not enough nerve to stand the racket that was coming upon them. Several other gangs tried to dig for it, but can not stand the ground long enough to find it. The spooks that were seen were of every description. One man saw a load of hay falling upon him, others see large dogs and different kinds of animals, such as are not liked to be seen. Last Monday night three of our men were digging for it, their tools consisting of an axe, pick, shovel, and digging iron, but did not proceed very far until the digging iron was bent round like a rainbow. It is supposed that the seal is now found, but not yet broken, as it is very hard to break.

The public road leading to Pleasureville would be what is now known as North Sherman Street. As noted in Chapter 1, this road actually connected to Toad Road at the time. This would have been the route, if traveling by land, from York City to Codorus Furnace. It was almost a straight shot northeast from Pleasureville to Toad Road - and a distance of only four or five miles, depending on where Toad Road started - and they likely made no distinction between the one road's end and the other road's beginning at that time.

So, here is this story of not just buried treasure on the road to Codorus Furnace, but *spooks* as well. "Spooks", in Pennsylvania newspapers, could mean anything from a ghostly apparition to what seems - by their description - to have been bigfoot creatures. Anything frightening and unusual could be termed a "spook" in the old Pennsylvania papers.

Again we have a note of large dogs in the area. As with so many of these old articles, there is a frustrating lack of detail, and we must wonder today what the reporter meant by animals "such as are not liked to be seen." Given the other things reported in the area, it seems we have a wide selection of the unusual from which to choose! Likewise, I wonder what the man saw when the "load of hay" fell upon him. Could something large and covered with long hair be mistaken for a load of hay in the darkness of night or in the panic of fear?

During one of my conversations with Christine (see Chapter 5), as we discussed some of the history and landmarks of the Toad Road region, she asked me if I had ever heard the stories of the lost silver mine in the area. I had not, nor had I told Christine about my fascination with the idea of buried treasure around paranormal phenomenon, as I had found the article above and thought it already checked the box, so to speak, for buried treasure in the locality. Unfortunately, Christine had very few details - it was just a story she remembered from her youth about a lost or forgotten silver mine near Toad Road.

There *are* silver mines in the greater region. The Pequea silver mines are not far away - just across the Susquehanna River in southern Lancaster County. The Pequea mines were thought to have been used by First Nations people before European feet touched these lands (though the mines were expanded and further used by French and German immigrants). Henry Shoemaker, the great Pennsylvania folklorist, recorded tales of lost silver mines in the mountains of central Pennsylvania. I have not heard other stories of silver mines anywhere in York County (there is, however, gold to be panned in some local creeks).

I am unsure if, geologically speaking, a silver mine in York County is even possible - though mining for silver and finding silver in said mine are two completely different things. Whether the mine was real or a half-remembered local legend, it makes little difference. It is a story of some sort of buried treasure beneath Toad Road - and another bit of strangeness to add to the pot of supernatural stew.

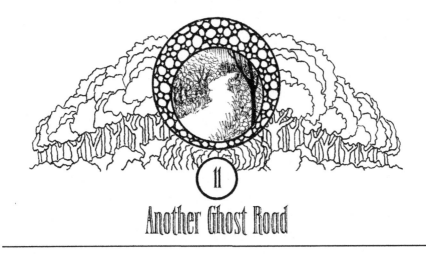

Another Ghost Road

Ghost Roads

On September 21, 2016, I was a guest on the popular radio program, Coast to Coast AM, discussing *Beyond the Seventh Gate*. In that volume I discuss, of course, Toad Road, and I mention some other closed roads as well. The host of the program, George Noory, asked an interesting question. He asked why there are so many closed roads in the areas about which I was writing. He commented that roads usually have a purpose - to go *someplace*.

I hadn't thought about this too much previously. Mr. Noory made a good point. There are usually fairly mundane reasons for road closures - in the case of Toad Road, it was washed out by Hurricane Agnes. Other roads I have written about were closed for various construction projects - or for repairs - and just never reopened. These roads did go *someplace* though, once upon a time.

Abandoned and forgotten spaces have always held an interest for me. I have always been fascinated by nature's reclamation of manmade structures and roads. It doesn't take long for grasses and weeds to push through the tiniest cracks in pavement or for vines to cover a house.

Abandoned and forgotten places also seem to be the kind of places which often attract The Other. If we are talking about shy or rare creatures, perhaps they simply populate those places where humans *are not* - or at least where we are not anymore. However, it isn't just cryptids (if you believe they are natural animals) which are said to hang around these places, but the whole range of paranormal phenomena. Countless ghost stories are attributed to abandoned houses and disused institutions (yes, like insane asylums). Towns across America have stories of sinister cults that meet in ruined basements, in old tunnels, or along forgotten roads. As mentioned previously, the Mothman of Point Pleasant, West Virginia was seen most often around the so-called TNT Area - which was peppered with abandoned munitions storage bunkers.

I started to take a keen interest in abandoned roads - particularly those roads near my residence. I began to visit and document these roads whenever I was able - and to find their stories whenever I could. I started calling these roads "ghost roads" - for they were themselves ghosts of older, often forgotten roads - overgrown and partially or fully lost to time. The fact that supernatural tales and sightings are so often associated with these places, gave the name "ghost road" further weight.

One ghost road yielded an interesting find. It was called by locals "The Cement Road" and ran through what is now Codorus State Park near Hanover, Pennsylvania. The park surrounds Lake Marburg, a manmade lake - known sometimes as "Project 70" (named after a Pennsylvania state land acquisition program from the 1960s, these various projects - including Lake Marburg - were all to be completed by 1970). Interestingly, Lake Marburg holds within its depths, the remains of the town of Marburg, flooded when the dam was built to make the lake. Of course, there are paranormal tales associated with Marburg. Lon Strickler tells of a frightening encounter with an apparition at this location (see *The Slave Woman of Lake Marburg* on PhantomsandMonsters.com).

One day in November of 2016, I followed the Cement Road through Codorus State park. This road passes by the old Manheim Union Burial Ground cemetery before it descends into Lake Marburg itself. The road visibly goes into one side of the lake and out of the other. I had to take the long way around and skirt the shores of the lake to resume my walk.

While not as overgrown as Toad Road, the corpse of the Cement Road is slowly being taken over by the surrounding woods. I followed the road northwest from its start at Landis Road in the south part of the park to somewhere in the middle of the park. It seemed to end at a large mound. As I glanced over the mound, something white caught me eye. It was a deer skull, sun-bleached white. I climbed over the mound to look at it. As I got closer, I noticed another skull, dark with lichen or some other stain, next to it - the two skulls reminded me of the Chinese yin-yang symbol. While I wasn't on a bigfoot investigation, I was there to document this ghost road, and I find it worth noting, that at its end, I should be greeted by skulls.

The yin-yang skulls as I found them.

Strange Things Seen and Unseen

Of all these ghost roads, Toad Road is my favorite. I am sure this is not surprising to my readers. It is my favorite for sentimental reasons; perhaps, because I wrote my first book about Toad Road - but also because there's just *something* about Toad Road that keeps drawing me back. I cannot explain it exactly, but the entire area seems to hold layers of history and mystery.

Because of my interest in the paranormal, in general, and Toad Road, in particular, I will often ask local folks if they have any knowledge or experiences in the area. I particularly like to ask people who are around my age or older because there is less chance that the outrageous "burning insane asylum" / Seven Gates of Hell legend is the story they will relate.

I thought Chris would be a great person to ask as he was from Columbia, Lancaster County (just across the river from Hellam) - and he was already interested in the paranormal. Chris has hosted ghost tours and collected many strange tales from Columbia and the surrounding areas. Besides the paranormal, Chris has an almost encyclopedic knowledge of local history - especially as regards Columbia - from the first residents to more recent events. Chris is a few years older than me, so chances were good that I wouldn't get a Seven Gates of Hell story from him.

To my disappointment, Chris wasn't familiar with any of the Toad Road legends, nor had he ever been there. The disappointment was only temporary, however, because Chris said he was familiar with *another* road in the area and proceeded to tell me some very strange things which happened at that place.

This road will remain unnamed in this volume. Like Toad Road, it is now closed. The road and the surrounding area is private property. My fellow investigators and I have given this road and the land that surrounds it a code name - Site 7 - so we can talk about it in public forums without giving away its location. The people who live around Toad Road are often tormented by legend trippers, trespassers, and thrill-seekers. I have no desire to create another such situation for the people who live near Site 7. Besides, our investigation of this area is ongoing.

Site 7 shares many features with Toad Road. It is a long-closed road which cuts through the Hellam Hills overlooking the Susquehanna River. Most of the area is wooded and not used much outside of hunting season. The road itself is surrounded by farm fields, high hills, and deep valleys where creeks cut through the landscape, heading toward the river.

Chris wasn't aware this road was closed when he told me about Site 7. He was in high school the last time he traveled the route. The first thing Chris told me, which caught my attention, was that if you stopped your car on a certain stretch of this road, "hobos" would throw rocks at your vehicle from the woods. I stopped Chris to clarify. "Hobos?" I asked. He affirmed. I followed up, "Did anyone ever actually *see* these hobos?" Chris said no, no one ever saw the hobos. I asked Chris if he had personally experienced this or if it was just a rumor he had heard. He told me that he had experienced this more than once.

Stone-throwing is a known bigfoot trait. It's really a known *paranormal* trait as it happens in poltergeist cases as well. However, when stone-throwing from an unknown source happens in the woods, it is often credited to bigfoot. It may, in fact, be more disconcerting if stones were thrown inside a residence or other structure as at least stones are commonly found in the woods. Where are the stones coming from that poltergeists are tossing inside houses? In both cases, bigfoot and poltergeist, the stones, when picked up, are sometimes found to be warm. Those who would like to eliminate any discussion of the paranormal in association with bigfoot, will simply say that the outdoor stones are warm because bigfoot creatures were holding them in their hands before throwing them - thus, they assert, the projectiles were warmed by the creatures' body temperature.

The next story of interest Chris told me about Site 7, was that there was a family of albino people who lived in a shack-like residence somewhere along the road. It was a strange detail that, at first, seemed like nothing more than a curiosity. Later, I would wonder if there wasn't something deeper and stranger associated with this albino tale.

Surely there would be some kind of record of a family of albino people in York County, Pennsylvania - or at least someone local should remember this family. Genetically speaking, though rare, it would not be impossible for a family of albino people to exist. There are records of a family with three children, all with albinism, as close as Harrisburg, Pennsylvania (though this was in 1889). I asked Chris if he ever saw the albino people. He replied that it was rare to see them - apparently they didn't leave their abode too often - but that he had caught glimpses of them once or twice.

There is some folkloric precedent for the family (or clan) of albino people living along a haunted road. Like the legend of the Seven Gates of Hell, the albino legend has sprung up in different states. Urban legend albino tales hail from California, New Jersey, Missouri, Nebraska, and - also like the Seven Gates of Hell legend - even other places in Pennsylvania. Among other terrors, Constitution Drive in Allentown is said to have a group of crazed albino people who will terrorize wary travelers. Who is to say where and when the legend first appeared? For whatever reason - and like so many other urban legends - the albino tales seem to have propagated across the country.

Hicks Road in San Jose, California is said to be the home of an entire colony of people with albinism. This colony is said to chase and attack people with weapons ranging from improvised clubs to shotguns. The most interesting thing about this legend is that some have discounted the stories of albinos and stated that the attackers are instead pale spirits of some sort.

I should take some time to state that the widespread urban legends of albinos are troubling at their core. I believe this is nothing more than fear of those who are different. There is nothing about albinism that would make people inherently evil or scary. Imagine if these legends were associated with people of *any* other skin color. The tales would be called racist, for sure, and that assessment would be correct. My interest in the "albino" tale, as regards Site 7, has only to do with people reporting things that are upright and white or light in color.

The entire section of the county which included at least some of the area that comprises Site 7, used to be called "Devil's Hole" by locals. There is still a place, somewhat close to Site 7, which is called Devil's Hole in modern times - this is the remnants of an old quarry along the Mason Dixon trail south of Wrightsville. It used to be that a much larger region of the county was known as Devil's Hole.

Certain people around here seem particularly sensitive to "devil" or "hell" names. Hellam Borough changed its name to "Hallam", for instance, because the citizens didn't want "hell" to be part of the borough name. Thankfully, Hellam Township did not give in to such childish ideas and kept the original spelling. So, perhaps it was this fear of the Devil that caused people to stop calling this section of the county Devil's Hole, or perhaps, it was more practical concerns. While it was never an official designation, it might be somewhat difficult to sell real estate in, or entice people to move to, a place called Devil's Hole.

Places which bear these "devil" and "hell" names are worth noting for our purposes. Bigfoot researchers have noted for decades that a disproportionate number of sightings seem to occur in places with "devil" or "hell" in the name: Devil's Creek, Devil's Pass, Hell Run, Satan Hill, etc. The list is long and extensive.

Is it possible these "devil" places were named after the things people were seeing there? Bigfoot were known as "mountain devils" in some places. Locally, the Susquehannock Indians were known to have images of the albatwitch on their war shields. Interestingly, some historical reports simply call the images on the shields of the

Susquehannocks, "devils".

David Paulides has written an entire series of books on people missing under mysterious circumstances called *Missing 411*. Paulides, an ex-police officer, was alerted to some of these strange disappearances by employees of the National Parks. As he looked into the cases of missing people, he found, again, what seemed to be a disproportionate number of the cases were coming from places with "devil" or "hell" names.

My research into the area led to another story, not far outside of what would have been known as the Devil's Hole region of the county. This is another tale of "spooks" from 1910:

Case of "Spooks"

A surety of peace case that aroused a lot of interest was the one brought against Solomon Rissinger, of Lower Windsor Township, by John W. Graham, for making threats to knock the latter's brain out. The parties live in the district known locally as Bull Run, a little community located in the hills that run back from the Susquehanna river at the foot of Long Level. The result of the suit yesterday was that Graham, the prosecutor, caught costs of prosecution, the case being dismissed by Judge Stewart. The trouble arose over the story that "spooks" were seen crawling over the roofs of porches. One night about the middle of June Rissinger thought he heard a noise on the porch roof just outside his bed window. He arose and investigated but found nothing to justify his fears. A day or so forward he met Graham and told him of his experience, and asked Graham who he supposed the marauder might be. Graham first suggested it might be another neighbor, David Ritz, but this suggestion was mutually abandoned, and Graham finally thought it might have been Rissinger himself. This Rissinger denied and taking Graham's taunt to mean that he (Rissinger) was doing the "spook" act, Rissinger called Graham a liar. Graham subsequently met Rissinger in front of the latter's house, and wanted to fight him, but Rissinger said he did not want to quarrel, but that if Graham would wait until he got his breakfast, he would go along down the road and talk it over. Graham told the court that Rissinger threatened to knock his brains out when the subject of "spooks" was first talked about between them, and that on a later day Rissinger was crouching in a fence corner with a handful of stones, lying in wait for him. Rissinger denied all of these charges.

(from *The York Daily*, September 26, 1905)

Our interest here lies not with a dispute between neighbors but with the idea of "spooks" and especially spooks crawling on roofs. As noted previously, "spook" is one of the terms often used in Pennsylvania newspapers to describe bigfoot and other anamolous creatures. There have been a number of reports - both modern and historical - wherein bigfoot witnesses report that the creatures have climbed upon their house and proceeded to walk or crawl across their roof. Of course, similar things are often reported in poltergeist cases - yet another trait shared between paranormal phenomena which are, according to most paranormal researchers, unrelated.

I cannot say if the "spooks" in the above article are supernatural or simply some sort of all-too-human neighborhood prowler. I simply find it interesting that a "spook" story which includes something crawling upon rooftops should occur relatively close to Devil's Hole / Site 7. To my knowledge the "spook" mystery at Bull Run was never solved.

Chris left me with a final word about Site 7 - he told me that he often got a feeling of "evil" when he traveled that road.

My interest was piqued. Another ghost road so close to Toad Road with so many strange and interesting tales! I couldn't wait to share the information with my fellow investigators.

Mysterious Lights, Greys, and Giant Weasels

Lori and Jeff (see Chapter 8) share my interest in bigfoot and other strange things, and we often compare notes on areas of interest and local sightings. I told Jeff about the stone-throwing "hobos" that nobody ever seemed to see at Site 7. He agreed that it was worth checking out.

Lori was actually the first of us to go to the area, as she lives closest. Her initial visit was in February of 2017. There were no leaves on the trees yet. She arrived in the area about dusk. There is a parking area on the west side of Site 7 where one can just get out of his vehicle and be surrounded on three sides by the woods while looking down the gated ghost road as it disappears in the trees.

We have found that if you just sit quietly in these places of interest, sometimes the strangeness will come to you. Many bigfoot researchers have made similar observations: It is better to just set up camp, sit and wait as opposed to wandering through the woods hooting and banging on trees with sticks.

Lori's first visit was rewarded with a sighting of mystery lights and orbs. One of these lights, which Lori referred to as an orb, came so close to her that she stepped back against her jeep in surprise. She started snapping photographs. Several of these photographs showed lights in the woods.

(Note: these photos and all the photos we have taken of the Site 7 light phenomenon are not reproduced here as they would look, at best, like pins of light on a black field. The photos are unimpressive and do the Site 7 lights no justice at all.)

Jeff sent me the photos with the comment that he thought they might be eyeshine. I gently pushed back at this idea, knowing there are all sorts of mystery lights, and I was not ready to weigh in so readily on the idea of bigfoot at Site 7. Time would show that Jeff may have been right from the start.

Eyeshine, or eyeglow, is one of the more difficult features of bigfoot reports. An incredible number of nighttime sightings report some sort of illuminated eyes on the creatures. Most often, the color is reported as red, but various other colors have been reported.

Many animals, especially those which are predominantly nocturnal, have reflective eyes. These creatures have what is called a tapetum lucidum - a reflective membrane behind the retina of the eye which reflects visible light. It would not be impossible to think of bigfoot having this reflective membrane in their eyes, especially since their eyes would be larger and, presumably, able to gather more available light.

However, even when there seems to be no available light, some people still report bright shining eyes on bigfoot creatures. This seems to be *eyeglow* as opposed to eyeshine, and it is a real problem in the bigfoot community. Those who would insist bigfoot are natural animals, also insist that witnesses are just incorrect in their observations; that what they are seeing is simply natural eyeshine - and that the witnesses simply didn't observe the light source which was reflected in the creatures' eyes.

For those of us who have seen these lights, and I count myself among them, this explanation will not do. The eyeglow, if that is what we are seeing, looks unnatural. It doesn't look like other eyeshine. These look like LED lights or something manmade. Indeed, I was somewhat certain I was seeing manmade lights myself, until they started behaving like no other lights I have ever seen.

Cryptids, across the board, seem to have this eyeglow, as do strange creatures in folklore tales worldwide. What is the purpose of glowing eyes? It would seem, to me, to be almost counter-intuitive to night vision. A light source within or close to the eye would obscure objects, not reveal them. Perhaps these things see in a different spectrum, and these colored lights in some way aid their vision?

In any case, mystery lights would become an ongoing feature of Site 7. Jeff has seen them so many times that he seems almost matter-of-fact when he discusses the lights. Whether they are eyeshine, eyeglow, strange orbs, or something else, is still up for debate.

One night, Lori visited the area and decided to leave an apple on the gate which closes access to the old road. This sort of "gifting" is somewhat common in the bigfoot community - and sometimes controversial as there are those who claim the bigfoot may come to rely on human food. I would argue that this kind of food gifting has its roots in far older folkloric practices. People often left food and/or beverage offerings to faeries, forest spirits, and other unseen beings.

Lori wanted to see if something would take the apple. When she got out of her jeep, she already had a creepy feeling. That eerie feeling of being watched by something unseen. She quickly left the apple upon the gate and climbed back in her jeep where she felt somewhat safer. After a time, she decided to leave. She started the jeep and put it into reverse. Illuminated by her reverse lights, in her rear view mirror, she caught a glimpse of something run behind her car, from right to left.

Lori was somewhat hesitant in her description. She said "I didn't get the impression that it was a bigfoot - or anything covered in hair". She said it was upright and white-grey in color. Her impression was that it looked more like the typical descriptions of so-called "grey aliens", or "greys" as they are also known. She turned herself around to see if she could get another glimpse, but whatever it was, had disappeared from view. She quickly turned her jeep around and left the area.

Lori and Jeff continued to make somewhat regular visits to Site 7. On one occasion in early 2017, they hiked into the area, via the closed road. They were in for a strange day indeed. At some point in their hike, a small log or large tree branch seemed to be thrown in their direction. They didn't feel it was thrown at them, but just near them - perhaps to get their attention or to warn them away from the area? They believe it was thrown, and did not fall, because the trajectory of the log or branch seemed to cause it to bounce through the leaves with forward momentum, two or three times, upon impact. They felt if the branch had just dropped from a tree, it would not have had the same kind of momentum.

As they proceeded, Jeff caught a flash of movement from the corner of his eye. He thought he had scared up a deer, but it turned out to be something far stranger. Most everyone who has investigated Site 7 has reported, at one time or another, a flash of movement: something so fast that it catches the eye, but disappears into the darkness or the brush with such speed that the witness is left unsure exactly what he just saw. This description "I saw a flash" was used so many times that some listeners to my podcast, *Strange Familiars*, thought we were discussing flashes of light when we talked about Site 7. We had to begin clarifying that we were talking about flashes of movement.

Lori got a better look at whatever this creature was, as it ran in front of her across the hill. It was quadrupedal, but did not move like a deer. Instead of the kind of bouncy up and down running of a deer through dense brush, this animal glided smoothly across the ground. She estimated it to be about 150-200 pounds, covered in brown fur, and a little bigger than her dogs. Lori owns two rather large Mastiffs - which makes this whatever-it-was quite big, but still shorter than a full grown deer at the shoulder. When Lori described her sighting, she mentioned several times that she saw no ears atop the creature's head. The day she saw the creature, she made a drawing. It looked, proportionately, like a ferret or a weasel. Lori said that, indeed, she was reminded of a ferret when she saw the creature - but it was much larger. Several species of weasels are native to Pennsylvania, but none come close to the proportions of the creature Lori described.

Abandoned Houses

During this time, I had made several daytime hikes through Site 7 and its surrounding areas. At first I wasn't experiencing the kind of high strangeness Lori and Jeff were reporting, but I am happy to be in the woods, strangeness or no. I did notice some possible tree breaks and structures in these "early days", but like so many of these I have seen, I would have to place them in the "inconclusive" category.

I did find two abandoned houses on the eastern side of Site 7. One was a very old farmhouse. Black vultures have taken up residence in the attic, often perching in its open window, and more than once, scaring me as they emerged from the window, flapping their large black wings when I passed by. One can find old farmhouses abandoned throughout the county - and I'm sure the reasons they are left empty are often as mundane as they are sad - whether it's foreclosure or the fact that the houses are simply forgotten by surviving family members.

The second abandoned house was more curious. It was a

small Cape Cod style house, probably built in the 1950s or 1960s. I approached from the back, at first unsure if it was abandoned, or, if instead, someone just gave up caring for the yard. Some junk was scattered about - broken furniture, a beat up gas grill, and bits of trash - mostly bottles and cans. I approached cautiously through the high weeds. I didn't want to see the business end of a shotgun pointed at me if someone was living there.

When I was confident no one was around, I peeked in the windows. There was furniture inside the rooms and plates and glasses on the table. Children's toys were still lying about here and there. The ceilings had fallen in in places, so it was obvious no one was currently living there but it looked like, whoever did, just picked up and left some years ago. It looked as though they hadn't taken much with them when they left.

I don't know what would have made the homeowners leave. I suppose it would be easy to suggest that it was something nefarious or spooky that made them run screaming from the abode, given the nature of this book, but what the reality is, I cannot say. I just note that this place sits on the east side of Site 7. It's just another strange feature of the area; another unanswered question.

In the summer of 2017, James Kibler called me about a very recent local bigfoot sighting someone had reported to him. As we had talked for *Beyond the Seventh Gate*, he knew I was interested in any such things. Some interesting events from James' childhood, including his father's Toad Road story, had led to a lifetime fascination with The Other. James would become my sometimes podcast co-host and my partner in paranormal investigations.

At this time, James knew nothing about Site 7. However, the bigfoot sighting he collected was just a couple miles away and from a couple weeks previous. I filled James in on all of the Site 7 strangeness, thus far, and we made plans to investigate the bigfoot sighting and Site 7 together.

A Back Yard Bigfoot

Cindy was happily playing in her back yard. At four years old, she had few worries. A bright summer day meant that she could spend the day outside on the sliding board or in the sandbox or just running through the large back yard, as she had done so many other times. Her grandfather sat in the back yard, casually keeping an eye on the girl, but he was relaxed and confident of her safety. Cindy's parents had made the backyard a kid-friendly place. It was a great place for a four-year old to spend the day.

It was to her grandfather's great surprise that he saw Cindy run screaming past him and into the house. He assumed she must have run into a yellow jacket nest or stepped on a bumble bee - and followed quickly after Cindy to see what was the matter. He found the girl cowering inside and screaming about a "big hairy monster".

It would be easy to dismiss this as a young child with an active imagination - but Cindy's parents and grandparents knew her temperament and proclivities. She was not the sort of child to make up monsters - nor was she, previous to this day, easily frightened. Her grandfather took the child's fear seriously enough to retrieve his gun before returning to the back yard to inspect it.

Cindy didn't give too many details about her "monster" - and her parents didn't press her too hard to talk about what she saw. They did not want the girl to live in fear. What Cindy did describe was something standing in the shadows and trees at the back of her property - it was taller than an average man and covered in hair.

This is what Cindy's mother told James: that her daughter had seen a big hairy monster and she didn't know what it was - nor what to do about it. She didn't use the words "bigfoot" or "Sasquatch" - because she knew nothing about the creatures or related phenomena. Cindy and family were Asian immigrants. They hadn't heard of bigfoot - even as far as American pop culture goes - and they certainly hadn't been exposed to the idea that bigfoot are real creatures people are seeing all across America (and beyond).

In the course of James' questioning, Cindy's mother mentioned some other details. Their motion sensor lights around the house seemed to be going on and off all night long - and they never saw what was triggering them. They had also heard some unidentified screams and other odd sounds they couldn't explain coming from the nearby woods. Cindy's family had a large vegetable garden as well as several fruit trees in their yard. Fruit and vegetables were going missing from the vine, before they could be picked. Vegetables would be there in the evening and gone the following morning.

The most unusual feature of the bigfoot sighting is that it occurred in broad daylight and in a residential neighborhood. It used to be standard practice for bigfoot investigators to look for the creatures only in deep wilderness. In more recent times, a number of investigators have started finding that bigfoot creatures and sign were being seen closer to human residences than we ever thought possible. Sometimes uncomfortably close. Usually there is some way in or out of these populated areas in which the creatures are seen - a creek bed or a strand of woods that connects the neighborhood to a larger wilderness. Whether they are natural animals or otherwise, these creatures seem to prefer staying hidden.

A glance at Google Satellite imaging showed that, indeed, there was a wide avenue of woods that lead from the Susquehanna River - right beside Site 7 - almost directly to the yard where Cindy was playing. With but one rural road crossing and a slight patch of farm field to move through, someone - or something - could make its way from the river all the way to Cindy's house and keep relatively hidden. In fact, if one were to think of this wooded avenue in terms of a train track, Cindy's back yard almost looked like the "last stop on the line".

Our investigation revealed some interesting things. The first thing we noticed is that there was almost no fruit on the back side of the fruit trees. At a level much higher than I could reach, almost all of the fruit had been picked (I am just over six feet tall). The family reported that in past years, the back sides of the trees bore as much fruit as the front. Additionally,here was almost no fallen fruit on the ground around the trees.

Beyond the fruit trees were some large decorative evergreen trees. In the shadows of these branches was a deep ditch that ran along the rear of the property - presumably for drainage. At three or four feet in depth, it wouldn't hide even a human standing upright - but its width would accommodate three humans crawling abreast. Even something very large could hunker down in that ditch and stay hidden, day or night. Beneath the low-hanging limbs of one of the evergreens was a wide, cleared-out space. I crawled into this hollow, and even from a few feet away, James couldn't see me. We could both sit easily and comfortably in this area.

We found some other interesting things beneath those trees: the broken stem of a wine glass that had been shoved into the ground so only the round bottom showed, some sticks laid in odd patterns across the ground, and what I like to call a "maybe footprint".

Clear, defined bigfoot prints are incredibly rare. There are those who claim to find them every time they go out. Without casting aspersions, I can only say that this has not been the case for me. I have only ever found these "maybe footprints" - inconclusive at best. While it seems to me somewhat important that even these "maybe footprints" should be found on investigations or in areas of interest, they are not much to show people. I won't even show "maybe footprints" to most other bigfoot investigators, let alone skeptics, as they are not the kind of clear and conclusive evidence that people want to see. People want big clear "ah-ha!" type proof and this is, sadly, all too rare. I believe The Other deals often in this inconclusiveness. Blurry photos and smeared tracks are all part of the game it seems.

In any case, we found a large foot-shaped impression in the grass behind the fruit trees. It was about 15-16 inches long and a bit wider than James' boot. This "maybe footprint" would not be much on its own - but taken with everything else, it becomes a "maybe" piece of the puzzle.

Screech Owls, Monkey Chatter, and Unknown Speech

James and I began to visit Site 7 with some regularity. His schedule at the time allowed for more night visits, while my own allowed me to visit during the daytime as well. On our nighttime visits, we would usually arrive at 10:00 PM or so and stay until 1:00 or 2:00 AM. We would always bring recorders with us - and sometimes leave them overnight.

We would park our vehicle on the west side of Site 7 at the gated road and just sit outside in the darkness. Here we were surrounded by woods, except the road leading out, and in almost total darkness (there is some ambient light from a distant house further to the west). This is the area from which Jeff and Lori saw the strange lights, and where Lori saw the grey figure pass behind her jeep.

Most nights throughout the summer and fall of 2017, we were greeted with the sounds of screech owls. The owl sounds were almost constant - and appear across most of our recordings from that time. While these owls sounded like nothing more than natural screech owls (whose warbling calls are much more pleasant than their names would suggest), due to the association of owls with all manner of paranormal activity, I would be remiss not to mention them.

Bigfoot creatures are said to be excellent mimics - people have heard everything from their own names and the names of their pets being called, to, remarkably, the sound of automobiles or other machinery all issuing from the woods where bigfoot are suspected to prowl. The thing bigfoot is most often reported to mimic, however, is owls. Often people will relate that the owls in question just sounded a little "off". As noted previously, sometimes you will hear witnesses tell of what sounded like a "800 pound owl" calling from the darkness. Other times, however, the creatures are said to mimic the sounds with near perfection (One wonders, in this case, if it is not simply owls and not bigfoot making owl sounds; but, alas even the proximity of natural owls to bigfoot or areas suspected to hide bigfoot, would be very much worth noting).

In the darkness, things could get very creepy indeed at Site 7. Sometimes we would hear knocks from the woods. Odd cries, random screams, and unidentified yelling were less common - but still present. Some of these cries could be explained away as foxes, owls, coyote, or other wholly natural animals - but some others, including some we captured on digital recorders, do not seem to fit the profiles of known Pennsylvania wildlife.

The most disturbing sound at Site 7 - and the most difficult to get used to - is what seems to be the sound of something (or things) which seems to walk around us as we sit or stand in the clearing. In the summer, when the leaves are thick on the trees and flashlight beams only penetrate a few feet into the wood line, these footsteps seem to come closer and closer. They often stop if someone speaks, only to continue some minutes later.

As I listened back to one of our recordings, I could hear something which sounded like a stone clearly 'ping' off of my jeep. I excitedly sent the audio clip to James who replied, somewhat casually, "Yes, I heard it hit the jeep that night. Didn't you hear that?" I had not!

The recorders we left on site often picked up interesting sounds. In one segment, which occurred at about 2:00 AM, you can hear a whole series of sounds. First, there is the sound of a distant car horn which is followed by what sounds like a wood knock. About 20 seconds after the wood knock, comes something which sounds like monkeys or chimpanzees chattering when they get excited.

On another recording, this time from a little after 3:00 AM, there is the sound of a voice - or voices - yelling. To my ears, it sounds like one voice, but James believes there is a second voice that answers the first. James describes these voices as sounding a bit like deaf people speaking - a description which has been applied to some reported bigfoot vocalizations as well. I describe it simply as an "unknown language" - for it sounds like language to my ears, but I cannot make out the words.

It is possible that a person - or people - happened by at 3:00 AM - on a closed road, marked private property - and started yelling for one reason or another. I would wonder at their reasons for being there. The recording in question was taken in summer, so early-rising hunters are not a likely explanation. However, we did meet some people one night at Site 7.

The Drone

It was late summer of 2017. James and I were sitting in the clearing at the gate of Site 7. I don't remember it being a particularly active night as far as unusual sounds - but I do remember it being a particularly *creepy* night.

From the time we arrived, I kept complaining to James that I just had a bad feeling. Something didn't feel right. It was quieter than usual - the screech owls and night insects seemed less active. They were there, but the usual chorus of nighttime noise seemed somehow dulled.

I told James that I felt like there were people in the woods, watching us. *People*, not bigfoot. My mind shot to Chris's story of the albino family, and soon I was crafting all sorts of scenarios involving angry hillbillies dragging us off to hidden shacks or white haired axe-wielders chasing us through the woods. It seems laughable now, but in the darkness, with the hairs raised on the back of my neck, I started to wonder: "What if these were more than just stories?"

Imagine how my heart dropped when, at almost precisely midnight, we saw lights in the woods. For a few seconds we thought

Jeff's and Lori's "eyeshine" was coming to greet us, but we soon realized the lights were flashlight beams.

I quickly tried to reason who would be there and why - thoughts of urban legend attackers quickly turned into more practical worries: poachers. If it was poachers, they likely wouldn't take too kindly to being greeted by two guys with a bunch of recording equipment as they came out of the woods. I suggested we get in the jeep and leave the premises.

I hadn't driven more than a few hundred feet when James said "No. We left a recorder out there. They aren't getting that recorder, whoever they are." Not wanting to be the coward, I spun the jeep around quickly, and we returned to the gate.

We saw no lights and no people. James jumped out of the moving jeep, like a man on a mission, and ran toward the gate. I put the jeep in park and followed him, one hand on the knife at my belt. By the time I got there, James was speaking to the darkness. "What are you guys doing?" he said, in a slightly bemused tone. This one phrase seemed to lift all of the tension in the air at once.

Crouching in the weeds behind the gate were three young men - older teenagers by my reckoning. "We thought you were cops," one of them replied. Assured that we meant them neither harm nor arrest, they came out of the weeds and into the clearing.

We exchanged some brief pleasantries and asked them what they were doing there, at night. They replied that things in the woods were just more exciting at night. Obligation to our investigations required that we ask them if they had seen anything strange back there.

An instant and almost breathless reply excitedly issued from one of the fellows: "You mean like bigfoot?!"

One of his partners shot him a stern look, as if to say "shut up!", then spoke up quickly: "No nothing like that. The only weird thing we saw was that drone you guys were flying over our heads."

We informed them that we didn't have a drone and they reacted with disbelief - for our position seemed to be the only logical place from which someone could fly a drone. After much reassuring and showing them we had no drone remotes or related equipment, they shrugged and walked off (one of the teens lived in a nearby residence).

Who was flying a drone, through the woods, on a dark summer's night, with thick leaves obscuring the view perhaps more than the darkness? If it wasn't a drone, what was it?

Earlier in the summer of 2017, a large UFO was seen hovering over the river, just north of Site 7, by multiple witnesses from both sides of the Susquehanna River. It was described as the size of a huge airplane with white and red lights on the bottom. The shape was difficult to make out, according to one witness I talked with, but the spacing of the lights suggested something the size of our largest jet airplanes, only hovering low over the river.

Later, in the autumn of 2017, I was driving just north of Site 7, on the way to a friend's wedding, when my wife called my attention to something in the sky. First one, then another craft of some sort glided low, heading from the west to the east. It was still daylight, and we saw no lights. These crafts were dull grey in color - and my estimation was that they were about the size of an average automobile. Their structure looked complex - more like a spaceship from Star Wars than a streamlined military drone. I am not eliminating the possibility that these craft were some sort of drone - military or otherwise - but they were unlike any I have ever seen in person or in photographs. These drones - or whatever they were - followed one directly behind the other, flew out over the Susquehanna River, and appeared to make a hard turn - they turned on a dime at a 90 degree angle - and headed southward down the river.

I don't know if either of these events - the UFO reported by multiple witnesses - or the drone-like things my wife and I witnessed - are in any way related to the "drone" our nighttime adventurers reported hovering over their heads that night at Site 7. However, as we are cataloguing the unusual in the area, these nearby sightings seemed worth mentioning.

As to our brave night hikers - one thing I noticed about them that evening was their clothes. Gym shorts and tennis shoes don't make great hiking gear. They weren't wearing high socks - in fact, they didn't appear to be wearing socks at all (That's a great way to get both ticks and poison ivy). They weren't really carrying any equipment except flashlights. They seemed incredibly ill-prepared for a hike - especially one over dark and rough terrain.

A short while later, a daytime hike revealed what was most likely their "party spot" - a couple old car seats, empty soda cans, and some junk food wrappers sat a few feet off of the old road - and perhaps a hundred yards from the gate. It looked like they weren't going far into Site 7 - just far enough to get out of view of any prying eyes. Their attire as well as their presence at Site 7 made much more sense after finding what I assume was their not-so-secret hideout.

We've made multiple visits to the area since that time and have never run into another human soul, including our teenage friends. Perhaps we scared them? Or perhaps they just don't go to their "party spot" too often?

As we drove away from Site 7 that night, James said, "Well, you were right." I thought he was perhaps chiding me for my earlier trepidation or the fact that I jumped to conclusions about who I thought was stalking us from the trees, but I asked him what he meant anyway. James replied, "There *were* people in the woods tonight."

More White Things

The stories of the albino family which supposedly lived along the road that cut through Site 7 would take new meaning over time. While Lori had reported seeing the light grey or white-ish colored entity, we didn't connect this to the stories of albino people at first. It was only after we started seeing other white things, that the albino story started taking on a different meaning.

On one of our first nighttime visits to Site 7, James and I saw something. We quietly exclaimed in an excited whisper to each other: "Did you see that?!" We both agreed we saw something large move from left to right across the old road, just beyond the gate.

Whatever it was, moved quickly and silently. We both saw it above a low-hanging branch which we would later measure at almost seven feet off the ground - making whatever we saw eight or nine feet in height, at least.

Our surprise and perhaps the thrill of the moment kept us from comparing notes at that time, but later James would ask me to describe what I saw. I told him I saw something above the branch. Something large, fast-moving, and silent. James agreed but followed up with another question. "Yes, but what *color* was it?" he asked.

I replied that it was white in color. James concurred. It was James who then pointed out the connection to these white and grey-white entities that were being seen and the old story of the albino family that was associated with the road. These are the kinds of connections that seem to creep up in paranormal investigations. They never cease to send chills up my spine and stir the fires of amazement within me. Sure, maybe it's just a coincidence, but, if so, what a coincidence it is!

It has been suggested by some who have heard the story that we simply saw a large white owl that night, and nothing more. To this I can only reply that whatever it was, crossed less than 20 yards from us, and it did not resemble an owl to either James or me. It is very easy to tell people what they "actually saw" when you were not there to witness it yourself. That said, I leave all possibilities open because we cannot tell you exactly what we saw. It was a flash of movement which caught our eyes, and whatever it was disappeared into the shadows before we could discern much more than its color and the height at which we saw it move.

When I listened back to the recording of that night, I was excited to find that it picked up the moment we saw the white flash of movement shoot across the road. I could hear the excitement in our hushed voices as James and I confirmed to each other that we had seen the same thing. I listened more closely to see if I could pick up anything unusual - perhaps footsteps or some kind of vocalization that wasn't ours.

After several listens, I realized there was indeed something strange about this recording. The *lack* of other sounds. There were no crickets or cicadas or any of the usual chorus of night insects which sang from almost every moment of our other Site 7 recordings. Even the almost incessant screech owls were dead quiet. There was silence, except for James and me.

A huge number of witnesses to the paranormal report the woods going silent directly before their encounter. It is one of the many troubling aspects for those bigfoot enthusiasts who would like to think of the creatures as relict hominids or undiscovered apes. Even the insects go quiet. The whole woods often fall silent in the presence of these creatures. The silence on the recording doesn't confirm we saw a bigfoot that night - or anything paranormal - it's just another small puzzle piece that seems to fit into a much larger puzzle. A puzzle to which we have not been given all the pieces; nor do we know how many pieces exist.

As the summer of 2017 faded into early fall, James and I decided to spend the day hiking through Site 7. We started at the Susquehanna River and made our way along various trails, and through thick brush, pushing up the steep hills (I think the hill in question may technically be a mountain, but just barely), and eventually hooking up with the ghost road that cuts through Site 7.

The first thing we noticed was, like Toad Road, large trees

seemed to be laid across the road every 30 to 50 yards. Whether felled by the weather or some other agency, these trees would insure ATVs, snowmobiles, or other motorized vehicles could not be used on the old road. One of the trees was so large that we had to climb through its branch network to proceed up the road. I had to snap the branches off and basically make a hole large enough to fit my pack and myself while James waited on the other side. (James wisely carries a much smaller pack!)

The hike up continued mostly uneventfully. We noted the locations of side trails and creeks and admired the excellent view of the river from our elevated position. After a few hours of exploration, we decided to head back to the jeep and call it a day.

We were casually making our way down the ghost road, having an easy conversation. The way back to the jeep was long but, quite literally, all downhill. We had done the hard work getting up there - or, so we thought.

The section of the road on which we were walking had been cleared of trees - the woods are some 20 or 30 yards from the side of the road - so there were wide open skies above us. Thick banks of brush grew to the very edge of the road, however - with all manner of weeds and high grasses tangling into what seemed to be an impenetrable wall of foliage some five or six feet high.

I heard the slightest sound in the weeds to my left. A quiet rustle. Just enough sound to make me turn my head. As I turned, I saw what I first took to be a man in a grey sweatshirt with the hood up; the kind of light heather-grey sweatshirts popular in the 1970s. The figure stood about 15-20 yards from us in those thick and tangled weeds. It was autumn, but just barely, and it was a hot day. The sun was beating down on that hillside making for a sweaty hike. My first thoughts were "Why is that guy staring at us - and why is he wearing a hoodie in this hot weather?"

As quick as those thoughts registered, and before I could direct James' attention to our observer, it turned to its left and ducked into the weeds, crashing off into the woods behind. James heard it running away but turned too late to see it. I say "it", but this entity could have been a "he" or a "she". It could have been human. I only saw the head and shoulders. The being, whatever it was, looked to be about my height, six foot or so. The proportions were not immense. The brevity of the sighting left me with no particular impression of a face. I only caught the shape of something upright and its color. Whatever it was, was grey-white.

Even if this was "only" a human, I am left with many questions, What was he doing there, on private property, where no one is supposed to be? Why was he observing us? If he was trying to stay hidden, why wear such a light color? Why was his hood up on such a hot day? Why wade in those thick weeds? Upon being seen, why not acknowledge us or stop and talk even? Why run?

Whether we were just overexcited by this sighting and making more of the normal sounds of the woods than usual, I cannot say, but we seemed to hear further sounds in the brush to our left as we made our way down the hill. Were we being paced out of the location, as so many bigfoot witnesses have reported elsewhere? If so, whatever was pacing us was being careful and as quiet as possible - it was not crashing along making itself known - which seems to be the case in many of these "pacing" bigfoot reports.

When we got to the large fallen tree I mentioned previously, the hole I had created to crawl through had been blocked off with a large branch. James said he thought the branch was there before, but as it blocked the hole I had made, I disagreed. In any case, it was easily removed and we made our way back down the hill.

To get back to the trails that would lead us to our starting place at the river, we had to cut through a brushy area and then a small strand of woods. I estimate it to be about an acre or less of woods in this section. As we pushed into the woods, nothing looked familiar.

I am not a forest ranger or the world's most experienced

outdoorsman, but I grew up on a farm, surrounded by woods. I spent my childhood in the woods. I hike often. I actually hike in these very woods often. James is not an inexperienced woodsman either. It was only a small strand of woods. We knew the river was east of us. We should have easily navigated those woods. We did not.

James and I spent well over an hour rambling through woods that should have taken us ten minutes to cross. The game trails we used to take us through previously, now seemed to twist around with no reason and dead end in patches of thorn or thick tangles of vines and brush. We didn't say much, but we exchanged confused looks quite a few times. I'm sure each of us was too proud to say we were lost - especially *there* in that little bit of woods - but we *were* lost. We could even hear a nearby road, and, occasionally, passing traffic.

We wandered around, confused, tired, and half stunned. "Wait, we passed that tree before … I think." "We already tried that trail!" Confusion turned to a kind of dazed irritation. Eventually, we stopped trying to reason our way out, chose a direction, and stayed the course. Finally, we came upon a trail I knew and made our way back to the river.

I didn't think too much of this part of the day at that time - I was too stunned and amazed having seen something else that was grey-white at Site 7. It was Joshua Cutchin who highlighted this last part of our hike as something more than just being lost.

"You were *pixie-led*!" Joshua said, after I told him the story. He went on to explain that similar stories are well-documented in tales of the fae folk. In those regions where "fae" or "faerie" was the name given to The Other, when people got lost in the woods - especially woods they otherwise knew well - they were said to have been pixie-led. The pixie-led often report being confused, tired, or almost in a haze. Sometimes they could even hear the voices of friends or family members, but still could not find their way out of the woods, just as James and I could hear the passing traffic.

I now blaze trees if I leave the trail, no matter where I am, but especially at Site 7. It was unsettling being lost like that, even with James by my side. I don't know how things would have worked out had I been alone. Tired and frustrated, would I have just sat down? What then?

Some days after our hike, James was describing the general weirdness of Site 7 to his sister-in-law. When he told her about the multiple sightings of white or light grey creatures, she stopped him, somewhat surprised. She recalled a sighting from her youth, on a busy road. A road which in fact lies between Toad Road and Site 7.

It was the early 1990s. Her parents were driving on the road in question when they saw multiple creatures descend from the north side of the road, cross to the south, and jump over a bridge. She hadn't thought about this sighting for a long time. She was a young girl when it happened - but she said there were at least three creatures, and perhaps four. They were large - human-sized or bigger - moved with great speed and were unlike any other animals they had ever seen. Her parents pulled the car to the side of the road and looked over the bridge to try to catch sight of the creatures. They weren't the only ones. Several other drivers had pulled over and exited their vehicles in order to view the entities. It was to no avail; they had disappeared.

While some of the details about the creatures James' sister-in-law saw were lost to time, there was one detail about which she was definite:

They were white.

Lights in the Woods, Eyes in the Lights

Our visits to Site 7 continued throughout 2017. Sometimes our visits would yield nothing remarkable. Other times, we might hear an unidentifiable vocalization, a single "whoop" from the wooded hillside, or a strange whistle; perhaps we might see an interesting tree structure or find a solitary cairn. However, as I have come to expect when attempting to gather evidence of The Other, it was all inconclusive.

Even in my own mind, after having experienced so many strange things at Site 7, and taken reports from others who had their own unexplainable experiences at the locale, I still had doubts. As I put time between myself and whatever weirdness I witnessed, questions would start to creep into my mind. Maybe we had just seen something white - something perfectly natural, but white. Maybe all those sounds we recorded were just natural sounds after all. Maybe James and I simply got lost in the woods that day. When you are not *there*, it becomes easier to "reason" The Other away as misidentified but wholly natural animals, sounds, and the like.

Doubt creeps in by the light of day or in the comfort of home - and the weirdness of events fades from shock and disbelief into just a memory of something that happened. The edge is dulled a bit by time. Sometimes I would think "maybe we have made too much of this Site 7" - or wonder if our expectations weren't somehow fueling our experiences there.

Jeff was steadfast. He was insistent. Not only were unusual things happening there, but they were happening somewhat dependably. Those strange lights Jeff witnessed on his early visits - they were there, in the woods, almost every time he visited. Jeff was also certain they were bigfoot eyeglow. "I've seen them walking around," he told me, speaking of the mysterious lights.

One night in February of 2018, I visited Site 7 determined to see Jeff's eyeglow. I would not be disappointed. James Kibler, was unable to accompany me on this night. Another friend and bigfoot investigator came with me, James Rester, who for brevity and clarity, I will refer to in this text as J.R., going forward.

It was about 10:00 PM when J.R. and I arrived at Site 7. It was pitch dark and chilly, but not frigid, luckily. We were able to comfortably stand outside and take in our surroundings. It took a half hour or more for our eyes to adjust to the darkness.

I started looking down the closed road, assuming incorrectly that was the area where Jeff was seeing the lights. As I saw nothing but blackness, I said to J.R., disappointed, "I don't know where these lights are that Jeff's been seeing." I assumed it would be an uneventful night.

A few minutes later, I happened to walk a few yards north of the gated road and gaze into the dark woods. Something in my peripheral vision caught my attention. A single light. It was white-blue and looked manmade. As I mentioned previously, it looked like an LED light.

"We have lights!" I said to J.R. in a hushed but excited voice. J.R. was incredulous, but walked over to have a look for himself. Until you see these lights, you are not exactly sure what you are looking for, and I believe this makes them more difficult to pick out at first. Of course, gazing through yards and yards of trees and hanging limbs means that the lights are often obscured. Moving around a bit, shifting positions, sometimes squatting or ducking down would sometimes reveal the lights' position.

At first it was just a single light - or so it seemed to be. We stared at it for some time, trying to reason what it might be. I knew the layout of the land, and I knew we weren't looking at a house. I thought it must be something manmade out there. Perhaps a light on a trail camera or some other piece of equipment someone left in the woods.

Then the light started moving and changing colors. It was a smooth but steady movement upward from its initial position. Sometimes it would gradually move back down. The color changes were more subtle. It did not blink and change colors like a Christmas light, but slowly blended from white to blue to green - sometimes going orange and yellow.

J.R. and I were both in disbelief and questioned each other several times. "It's moving, right? You see it moving, don't you?" "What color does it look like to you right now?" The light was behaving in a very odd manner. We wanted to confirm with each other that our eyes were not playing tricks on us.

Another light lit up to the left and down from the first light. Then another light beside that one. Some moved more than others - or would seem to blink out only to reappear in another area of the woods. I texted Jeff and told him "I see your lights." He texted back that he was on his way.

It is important for me to state that, at this time, I believed these were nothing more than lights - not eyeshine or eyeglow. Though they were moving and changing color, I was actually still somewhat confident that these were just manmade lights which were somehow appearing to do strange things.

That was before the laser.

J.R. had with him an incredibly powerful green laser pointer. I believe its distance was rated at 10 miles. Being the curious type I said to J.R., "See what happens when you hit those lights with that laser."

It took J.R. several tries, but eventually he was able to hit the first light we saw with the beam of the laser. When he did, the light turned red for a few seconds and then went black. It didn't blink out, but kind of drew down to black as if an aperture was closing.

No manmade lights, to my knowledge, react this way to a laser beam. Thirty seconds to a minute passed, and the light came back on, once again the blue-white LED color. I told James to hit it with the laser beam again. Again, the light turned red and apertured out. We repeated this process several times and with each of the lights. The results were the same: the lights would turn red for a few seconds, then black out, only to come on again a few moments later.

By this time, Jeff had arrived. He was still confident that we were looking at eyeglow. I simply couldn't reason how these lights could be eyes. When they moved in that smooth steady way, Jeff reasoned that was when the creatures were standing up from a prone position. When a light went out and seemingly lit up elsewhere in the woods, Jeff said it was the creatures moving from place to place. I told Jeff I wasn't sure I believed they were eyeglow. I told him I thought they were just some kind of weird lights.

From that moment, the night continued much the same. We tried the laser several more times with the same results. J.R. saw something large and black move across a ridge, somewhat backlit - but it was far away, and he couldn't make out any details.

It seemed that at least one of the lights was making its way closer and closer to us. Our attention would be drawn to the first lights, and I would look over and down for the light that seemed closest to us, and it would be gone. The next time I would look, I would see it shining, seemingly closer than it was before. I don't know if this encroaching light influenced our decision, but at some point, in unspoken agreement, we got in our vehicle and left.

It's hard for me to guess how big the lights were. I originally thought they were about grapefruit-sized. However, I also originally thought they must be 150 yards away, if not more. I was incorrect in that estimate.

A couple days after this experience, I hiked in to Site 7 alone, determined to find some explanation for the lights. I made the mistake of hiking in from a different location from where we had been standing, which made it difficult to know, for sure, if I was in the right place. I did find a massive tree structure on this day, however, in an isolated area, off-trail. The entire top of a very large tree had been jammed in the ground, top down, and stood straight, six to seven feet high. The trunk was the size of a telephone pole. Around this, were several other stick formations which looked to be created by something with hands. I looked around to try to see the tree which had lost its top - falling, spearlike, and impaling itself top-down in the earth. I found no obvious candidates nearby.

J.R. and I returned to the exact place, where we were

X-structure at Site 7 - photograph by James Rester.

watching the lights one day in the spring of 2018. The trees had leafed out, but we could still see through the woods in the direction of the lights. I was surprised by two things.

First, where we saw the lights was on the face of a hill. There was no chance that we were looking at some far-off lights which only seemed closer. We weren't looking *through* a hill.

Secondly, those lights were *much* closer than I had originally estimated. They were more like 50-75 yards away. Half the distance I had assumed. The light which seemed to be coming closer to us was probably only 30 yards away from where we were standing.

J.R. and I walked right up to the tree line that day, to try to get a better view. When we did, something vocalized. A kind of grunting bark seemed to come from the direction of the hill where we saw the lights. J.R. thought it could have been a fox. It could have been, but if so, what timing this fox had!

We also noticed something else - through the gap in the trees - right where we had been looking at those lights, just inside the woods, two tall trees were crossed to form a large X. Some bigfoot investigators say the X-shaped tree structures mean "keep out" - a kind of delineation between bigfoot and human territory. Who can say if they are correct? I thought it was interesting to find this X here, however, right where we had been standing and shining a very powerful laser at something. As time went on, I wondered more and more if Jeff was right: that something at which we were shining the laser beam - those weird lights - were they somehow the eyes of bigfoot? If not the eyes of bigfoot, were these lights somehow related to bigfoot?

In May of 2018, I was listening to an episode of *Sasquatch Chronicles* podcast (Episode 430: *Strange East Texas Encounters*) when I was shocked to hear a witness from Texas named Jeremy. He described lights he was seeing in the woods where he was experiencing sasquatch activity. He noted will-o-the-wisp type orbs, but also strange eyeshine or eyeglow associated with bigfoot activity. Jeremy mentioned that the eyes of a creature he saw not only glowed, but also changed color - from blue to green to white. What Jeremy was describing sounded very much like what we were seeing at Site 7. At this point, I became much more open to Jeff's declaration that the Site 7 lights are eyeglow.

I talked about the color-changing lights / eyeglow we saw on several podcasts, including *Sasquatch Chronicles* (Episode 434: *Strange Lights in the Woods*). Upon hearing my tale, I was chastised by more than one listener for having J.R. shine the laser in the eyes of bigfoot creatures. I must make it clear that, despite what Jeff was telling us, we in no way thought these lights were the eyes of bigfoot at this time. To J.R. and myself, they were simply weird lights.

Today, still not knowing exactly what the lights are, but leaning toward bigfoot eyeglow as one possible explanation, I would not point a laser at those lights. Even if they are not eyeglow, in hindsight, I feel like using the laser was kind of poking at the phenomenon, whatever it is. I don't think it's a good idea to try to provoke something, known or unknown, natural or supernatural. We will no longer be shining laser beams at weird lights.

Rare Things, Known and Unknown

One night late in July 2018, James and I returned to Site 7. Summer heat and familial obligations had kept me away from the area for some time.

To be honest, seeing those weird lights with J.R. had changed the way I thought about the area. Time would not deaden these memories. I could not reason these lights away as something manmade or natural that I had somehow misperceived. Those lights - whatever they were - did not behave like anything else I had ever seen, and they were absolutely real. Three of us saw them together; changing colors, moving, and going black when they were hit by the beam of the laser. The lights were real, and they made everything else we experienced feel all the more real as well. This somewhat dampened my enthusiasm for exploring Site 7 alone.

When James and I arrived, it was after 10:00 PM. The trees were heavy with leaves and the foliage thick with summer growth. The woods had closed in on the clearing more than we had ever seen them in the past. The night insects were singing in a clamorous chorus which made it hard to hear much else. Our vision and our hearing were both being stifled by summer itself.

We were greeted again with sounds of something walking through the woods - and with what sounded like distant voices, barely audible and indistinct. Loud enough to hear, but quiet enough to make you question what exactly you were hearing. The screech owls were conspicuously silent this night - whereas before we had heard them almost constantly, and on almost every visit in the warm months.

A new set of sounds which did greet us was a fast kind of tapping. It sounded like someone tapping a stick on a log; not a big loud cracking "wood knock" as bigfoot witnesses often report, but a repetitive tapping sound. This sound seemed to move around us - first we would hear it to our right; then behind us; then to our left; then in front of us. The tapping would sound for minutes at each location before going quiet, then starting up again in another place. At one point, late in our visit, the tapping seemed to emanate from just inside the wood line to our left. The tapping sounded like it was mere feet away. Branches hung low with leaves and cast deep black shadows which easily hid the tapper from our sight. I could not bring myself to lift the branches and shine my flashlight into the woods, so we simply listened until the tapping stopped again.

Though Jeff said he couldn't see the lights when leaves were on the trees, I was really hoping to show them to James. Focused on the hill where we saw the lights previously, I ducked and bobbed and crouched and leaned, all in an effort to catch sight of the lights. Eventually, I hit the right angle, and I saw one of the lights. Whether the lights were moving, or my own movements, however slight, changed the angle and obscured the lights, I cannot say - but the lights were hard to keep in sight.

Before anyone suggests that we were seeing fireflies, let me say that I know what fireflies look like. There are not fireflies in the woods in February when J.R. and I initially saw the lights. The lights we saw in July looked exactly like the lights we saw in February. They are neither the right size nor the right color to be fireflies.

Eventually, James was able to see the lights as well, however briefly. He was equally impressed, knowing what is (or more precisely, what *isn't*) in the direction we were looking. Just as J.R. and I had some months before, James wondered aloud, "What is that?"

We often stand facing each other at Site 7. This allows us to look over each other's shoulder and observe more of the area at once. Too often, our attention has been drawn to a sound in one area, and as we looked in that direction, trying to see, another sound would come from the opposite direction. We began to wonder if something wasn't trying to distract us, so we began facing each other, somewhat staggered in our positions, so we could observe more of the location at once.

We were standing in this position, when James called my attention to the west. There were two lights, side-by-side, like eyes, and they were in front of the ambient light from the distant house I mentioned previously. Again they moved - or blinked - or our position moved enough that the lights were obscured behind branches and leaves. For whatever reason, it was difficult to keep these lights in sight, but we did see them, several times.

We spent about two hours at Site 7 that night. Towards the end of our visit, things seemed to pick up. James was hit by a pebble or something pebble-sized. He felt it bounce off of his hat, but couldn't find the projectile in the darkness.

The feeling changed. This is very subjective and it's somewhat difficult to relate, but it seems to happen at some point in every one of our visits to Site 7. Perhaps we are just tired, but the wonder and curiosity seems to turn to something more ominous. Without speaking a word, it seems, everyone agrees it's time to leave. I cannot think of one visit to Site 7 where one of our party said they were not ready to leave. At some point, it's just time to go.

We had reached this point, but hoping to catch some sounds on tape, James and I decided to stay just a few minutes longer. We try not to turn on flashlights when we are doing night investigations because we use tactical flashlights, and the beams are so strong it takes several minutes for your eyes to readjust to the darkness after turning the lights off. At the end of our visits, we usually turn on the flashlights and just have a quick look to see if they illuminate anything of interest.

We resolved that the next unusual sound would spell the end of our night. We would turn on the flashlights, look around, and leave the area. We approached the wood line facing directly toward the hill where we saw the lights most often. We were greeted with a low groan. It sounded close, and it had the effect of backing James and me into the center of the clearing.

I turned on the flashlight, aiming in the direction we were looking. I saw nothing but branches and dark shadows. The light barely penetrated the woods. I panned the light across the trees to my right and, finally, past the gate and down the closed road. That's when we saw the eyeshine.

It was definitely eyeshine this time. Reflected in the beam of the flashlight were two large round eyes, gleaming yellow, and high off the ground. Whatever it was, turned away from the beam - I could see the eyes turn. We then caught another gleam of eyeshine as whatever it was seemed to turn and give another glance in our direction. As soon as the light caught them, the eyes turned again. These eyes were facing forward. If it was a natural creature, it was not a deer. If it was an owl, it was an absolutely massive bird.

The groan and the eyeshine were enough. We got in my jeep and drove away. As we drove on the rural roads leading around Site 7, something in the road caught my eye.

"What is that?" I asked James. It was small and quadrupedal but something about it just looked odd.

"I think it's a cat," James replied. I slowed the car, and we crept closer. The animal crossed in front of the car and climbed a bank next to the road. It wasn't a cat. It was hairless with long legs and big ears on either side of its head. It was about the size of a large domestic cat or a small dog. It was grey-brown in color and resembled a canid, but for the tail which looked more feline or even rat-like. Neither James nor I could identify this creature.

We got a long look at it as, whatever it was, stayed on the bank and looked at us for a minute or more as the car idled beside it. It didn't seem scared or upset that we were in such close proximity.
Eventually, it turned and slinked off into the shadows.

We were amazed at seeing this creature. What could it be? We wondered at the possibilities. Was it some exotic domestic dog we had never seen? Was it some other kind of cryptid creature, as yet unidentified? I drove James to his car at our usual rendezvous place, but we sat together for a time to try to sort out what this small creature could have been.

James typed "hairless fox" into an internet search, not thinking it would yield any answers. We were rewarded with an image that was almost exactly what we had witnessed. It was a hairless grey fox. These foxes are the result of a rare genetic condition which causes less than 1% of the population to be born without the guard hair. They are not so much hairless as very short-haired.

This fox was a perfectly natural creature. However, like the water moccasin found on Toad Road, it is extremely rare (At least, water moccasins are rare in York County). To my mind, as with the water moccasin, it is worth noting when something so rare, however natural and explainable, appears in these areas of interest - right alongside the other rare and not-so-easily explained phenomena.

No Answers

I have no explanations for what we have seen at Site 7. I can't imagine that a troop of bigfoot creatures lives there. There is simply not enough land at Site 7 to sustain such animals. What then? Do they travel through Site 7? If it is indeed bigfoot creatures we are dealing with, they sure seem to be there often. Why?

Is it simply The Other recognizing that we are looking for it, in whatever form, and putting on a show for us? Always staying two steps ahead of us. Never giving us anything conclusive. I wish I had an answer to any of these questions, but I do not. The game The Other plays is as frustrating as it is enticing - but one does not play to win. One plays only to experience the game.

We will continue to visit Site 7, but I do not expect answers will be forthcoming.

Appendix I: The Ghosts and Wild Man of Accomac

In all of my writing regarding Toad Road and the Hellam Hills thus far, I have only briefly discussed the haunted Accomac Inn - a historic property with roots dating back to the earliest European settlers of York County. The Accomac, as it is known locally, sits along River Drive in Hellam Township, less than three miles from Toad Road.

The ghosts of the Accomac Inn are supposedly John Coyle, the son of a former owner, and Emma Myers, the milk maid who spurned his marriage proposal. As the story goes, when Emma rejected John, he pulled a pistol and shot her dead.

John Coyle was tried and hanged for murder in Adams County. An article from 1910 relates some of the details:

Coyle Murder Recalled

An old style, rusty revolver exhibited in the window of R. S. Magee's hardware store at Wrightsville, recalls the murder of Miss Emma Myers by John Coyle in the barn that now stands at the Accomac pleasure resort, on the York County side of the river opposite Marietta. The crime was committed with this revolver thirty years ago. Coyle was hanged for the crime and his body reposes in an unmarked grave surrounded by a low fence almost within shadow of the barn where the murder was committed while the girl was in the barn milking one of the cows. Coyle, who had been forcing his attentions on her, entered the stable and because she refused to listen to his pleadings to become his wife he shot her three times. He was arrested and taken to York. Fearing that he would not get a fair trial because of the bitter feeling against him a change of venue was granted and the case was tried in Adams County court. Coyle was found guilty and paid the penalty of his crime on the gallows in the jail at Gettysburg.

(from *Adams County News* May 21, 1910)

The Accomac Inn - unknown photographer, from the author's collection.

Whether the reporting was incorrect or the stone was erected afterward, there is a marker on John Coyle's grave, which sits in the trees on the Accomac property. The epitaph reads: *Mother do not weep for me, for I am not dead, only sleeping here.* It is an interesting turn of phrase for someone whose spectre is said to still roam the grounds.

It is said that the Coyle family wished for John to be buried in Marietta but as he was a convicted murderer, his corpse was refused admittance to the burial ground. The family buried him on the property, close to the barn where he murdered Emma Myers. After his internment, John's father slept upon his son's grave for three nights in order to protect John's body from grave robbers.

The ghost stories of the Accomac have been well documented in multiple books of local ghost lore. Employees have reported feeling watched - or otherwise as if there is a presence in the room with them - spectres of a man, woman, and even a disappearing cat have been seen. Local ghost hunting groups have captured interesting EVPs (Electronic Voice Phenomena - unexplained voices captured on recordings - many times in areas reported to be haunted) - and unexplained music has been heard in the building.

As I looked for more information on the Accomac Inn, I found some other articles of interest from 1913:

See Wild Man

Marietta, June 16. — Considerable excitement prevails on the other side of the Susquehanna River, as a wild man was seen by a number of persons. He was last seen near the summer resort, Accomac, by one of the proprietor's daughters, when she ran into the house. Diligent search failed to locate him. The man was nude and had a long beard. Parties hunted all day for him.

(from *Harrisburg Daily Independent* June 16, 1913)

Wild Man at Accomac

Human Being, Entirely Nude, Inhabits River Hills — Chased Girl.

Accomac, June 16. — A supposed wild man was seen in the hills near here, on Friday, by a daughter of Leonard Waller, proprietor of the summer resort, at this place. She was badly frightened by his appearance.

While walking near the water's edge she observed the bare foot of a human being, and upon approaching it, a man, entirely nude, arose and chased her into her home. A search was made immediately, but no one could be found until several hours later, when a man was seen walking down the path and was ordered to leave by Mr. Waller.

Yesterday he was seen in the hills by several visitors from the lower end of the county, who spent the day there.

(from *The York Daily*, June 17, 1913)

"Wild" Man Reported

A "wild" man is reported in the hills near Accomac, across the Susquehanna from Marietta. He is said to be nude and to have long beard and hair. It is believed he is an escaped lunatic.

(from *The Courier*, June 22, 1913)

I have now compiled two full books of what I believe to be historical bigfoot sightings (*Bigfoot in Pennsylvania*, and *Bigfoot: West Coast Wild Men*). Before "bigfoot" and "Sasquatch" were common terms in our culture, people were still seeing large, hairy, upright-walking things in the woods across America. The newspapers most often reported these entities as "wild men".

Sometimes the creatures were reported as, instead of being covered with hair, having long beards and / or long hair which reached the ground.

Often it is difficult by the descriptions to tell if the "wild men" in the articles were indeed bigfoot creatures or simply homeless people, itinerants, or others that simply fall outside the purview of "normal" society. Such is the case with the Accomac wild man reports. However, given its proximity to Toad Road, these articles are interesting to say the least. The fact that the Accomac proprietor's daughter was "badly frightened" by the appearance of the wild man would suggest that, perhaps, it was something stranger - and scarier - than a naked human who pursued her.

How strange it is that the son of one of the previous owners of the Accomac killed a young woman on the property, and years later a daughter of another proprietor is chased by a "wild man"! Another case of multiple weird things occurring in one area: murder, restless spirits, ghostly animals, strange music, and a wild man all surrounding one property in the Hellam Hills, so close to Toad Road.

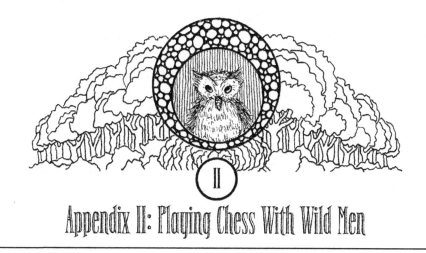

Appendix II: Playing Chess With Wild Men

Pull the Threads

How can you write about other people's experiences and not write about your own?

It was a valid question, asked to me by Mike Clelland during a shared appearance on the *Where Did the Road Go?* radio show. I didn't really know how to answer at the time. I hadn't given it a lot of thought at that point.

My experiences seemed so personal to me. With reflection, everyone's experiences are personal to themselves. I hold no unique position on that front. People were opening up to me about very strange sightings and unusual events. Was I being selfish in not sharing my own experiences?

More than this, as I related in my introduction, so much of this stuff just sounds *crazy*. I think I was holding back my own experiences in some effort to appear, perhaps, less crazy. "I just write about weird stuff; I'm not a *weirdo*." Of course, mainstream society doesn't see things that way. Simply being interested in the paranormal makes me a weirdo.

In my defense, my books thus far haven't really been the place to tell my stories. *Beyond the Seventh Gate* was about Toad Road and weirdness in the surrounding counties. At the time I wrote that book, my stories had little to do with this region. Likewise, my entire story starts with a very early UFO sighting, a Witch Tree, and some possible "alien abduction" memories - all of which started in Maryland, a long time ago - and fall outside the scope of this volume. (I have told about these things on various podcasts and in different pieces of writing that have appeared elsewhere - and someday, perhaps, I will find a way to collect all of these stories under one cover).

Since diving deeper into this world of liminal places and strange synchronicity, I have experienced unusual events that fall well within our areas of interest: shaking trees; hanging skulls; and everything that haunts Site 7. These stories I have included in the main body of the book.

In *Beyond the Seventh Gate*, I devoted some considerable wordage to the area of Hex Hollow. Besides being a nexus of paranormal events in its own right, Hex Hollow was one of the original supposed locations of The Seven Gates of Hell, which were later attributed to Toad Road, of course. This appendix will be devoted to a series of synchronicities and strangenesses I experienced in Hex Hollow. These events overlap in time, considerably, with the events I have related in previous chapters relative to Toad Road and Site 7.

Throughout this volume, I have taken Mike's advice and added my own stories to those of the witnesses. There is another bit of advice Mike gave me that night on *Where Did the Road Go?*: As regards all of this weird stuff I was experiencing, Mike said "Pull the threads."

I'm pulling, Mike. I'm pulling.

The Beginning

It started in summer 2016. One hot day, I was hiking with a friend in Hex Hollow and shards of white caught our eye. At the head of a trail, upon a boulder, were splinters of white quartz and white quartz rocks scattered all around. It looked very much like someone had been sitting there and smashing the quartz upon the boulder, again and again.

It was nothing more than an interesting scene to me. A curiosity. Without thinking about it too much, I stacked the quartz into a cairn atop the boulder. A short way down the trail there were two more boulders, one on each side of the trail. On one was an interesting collection of junk: rusted tractor parts; bottle caps; bolts; shotgun shells; and unidentified bits of rusted metal. On the opposite boulder, was a messy collection of stones. I moved the junk into what I felt was a more artistic arrangement, and made more cairns with the stones on the opposite rock.

For some reason, I was drawn to the area. There was something about it. I normally hiked in the area once to twice per week. I made this trailhead, with the white quartz, a regular part of my visits.

My next visit was no more than a week later. I found the cairns rearranged and more junk added to my assemblage on the other boulder. While I had read of bigfoot witnesses engaging in games of "rearrange the cairn" with creatures, at this time, I simply assumed it was people who were moving things around.

I repeated the process - changed the cairns, changed the arrangement of junk - and left. When I next returned, things were rearranged again. My interest piqued, I started to visit the area even more frequently - and almost every time I changed things, I would return to find them stacked or placed differently from the way I had left them.

Most often the stones would be left in triangular patterns - just three stones, each at the point of a triangle. The other stones would be cast about the area carelessly. The "junk sculpture" would change more subtly - but it did change. New pieces of metal would appear. Other pieces would disappear, only to be left on the boulder again days or weeks later.

Over time, I started making my cairns more complex. I figured if it was a human playing this game with me - and I did still believe it was a human at this point - then I would match the complexity of what was left. Instead, it was always simplified, and most of the time simplified into the three-stone triangle pattern.

"You know you're just playing a game with another person," my wife, Alison, ever the skeptic, said to me. I replied that I believed it probably was a person. Whoever they were, visited the area at least as often as I did, and I rarely saw another person on the trails. I was impressed with their dedication to our game. Alison began jokingly calling the area my "chessboard."

I continued my "chess game" throughout the summer and into autumn 2016. I was documenting each change of the stones with photographs. This became somewhat ponderous as I acquired photo after photo of cairns, all of which begin to look alike over time. However, since I would keep the photos of the previous visit on my phone, it was easy to look back and see exactly how I had left things - and how things had changed.

At some point in early fall, my children had a day off from school, and my family decided to go for a hike in the area. Alison walked with the kids on a lower trail while I went up to check the "chessboard." I rearranged things, took photos, and left to meet them at a designated location. When I got there, Alison asked to go see my "chessboard", so we headed back up the hill.

I had been gone for perhaps 15 or 20 minutes. When we

returned, I found a large oak leaf placed *under* one of the stones I had rearranged. Leaves do not fall under stones. I looked around in amazement. This is the first time I thought that it might not be a human I was playing "chess" with.

It was the middle of the day, during the week. Most people should have been at work or in school. We saw no other people in the area that day. We heard no other hikers. Our car was the only one in the parking area (granted there are other parking areas, so it's possible there were other vehicles in those locations). If it was a person who placed the leaf there, they must have been quiet and fast and they must have been watching me from a nearby location. I was stunned.

Another Inconclusive Encounter

The "chess" game continued into the winter months. One day in January of 2017, I made my usual hike to the "chessboard". There was a light dusting of snow on the ground and the woods were eerily quiet. I remember thinking at the time that I had never felt so alone there, even though I hiked the area by myself dozens if not hundreds of time. As I turned onto the trail that led uphill to the "chessboard", I heard from behind me what sounded like a rock clack: two rocks being hit together.

I turned and saw nothing but didn't think terribly much of the sound. Maybe it wasn't what I thought it was. Maybe it was something else, I told myself, as I proceeded up the hill.

The cold silence was cut by a murder of crows sounding a cacophony of croaks and caws as they took off from the trees and flew overhead. I noted this as unusual, for this group of crows often roosted in this section of the woods, and they were somewhat used to me. They would, on other days, alert to my presence with a few caws, but generally held their place in the trees.

Arriving at the "chessboard", I began to rearrange the cairns but I was overcome with a thick and heavy smell: a musky kind of skunk odor mixed with the stink of rotten flesh. I then heard what sounded like a wood knock - a heavy wooden branch hitting a tree. The sound came from the opposite direction from which I had heard the rock clack. The woods fell dead silent. I rose up from the cairn, suddenly overcome with an intense fear.

I had read and listened to enough bigfoot encounters to know what this meant: the smell; the silence; the wood knocks and rock clacks … I was about to see a bigfoot! I was in no way ready. My knees first buckled and then locked. I leaned heavily on my walking staff, feeling somewhat faint. Fight or flight instinct kicked in and I chose flight in my mind, but my legs would not move. I tried to steel myself.

"This is what you have been searching for, isn't it?" I told myself. The silent pep-talk did little good. If I could have teleported myself to safety in that instance, I would have.

As the fear built to a state of near-panic, I heard another sound I cannot explain. From the direction of the wood knock, came a sound like metal gears turning: click - click - click …and then nothing.

The smell went away. The fear went away. The natural sounds of the woods seemed to turn back on in an instant. I was able to rearrange the cairns and even stayed in the area for a short time to collect myself, though I could not work up the nerve to walk in the direction of the wood knock and the metal clicking.

I turned and retraced my steps down the hill. About halfway down, I noticed what looked like tracks in the snow. They were about 16 inches long and almost six inches in width. There were four footprints that came out of a wide game trail, across the trail I was walking, and into a cornfield on the other side. There was about a five-foot stride between each print. I could not follow the footprints back further than the mouth of the game trail as the trees had kept much of the light snow from settling in the woods - the leafy detritus only helped disguise the impressions. Nor could I follow the tracks through the cornfield. Though the corn was cut, the stalks and rough ground made it difficult to see where the next track landed.

I could not make out individual toes in these prints. They would probably not impress other bigfoot investigators, much less convince a skeptic. I can only say they looked like large bare footprints in the dust-covering of snow. More "maybe footprints". I did not notice these on the way up to the "chessboard", but that doesn't mean they were not there at the time. I am often saying one phrase about paranormal evidence, and I repeat it here regarding these footprints: Of course they were inconclusive. I should expect nothing more or less.

Wizards and Wild Men

It was shortly after that last experience that I told my saga of the "chessboard" to Seriah Azkath, Mike Clelland, and Joshua Cutchin on the *Where Did the Road Go?* radio show / podcast. I had, at that time, purchased, but not yet read Mike's book, *The Messengers*, though I had listened to Mike interviewed on many different podcasts and watched YouTube videos of his presentations. I usually have a stack of books in my "to read" pile, and Mike's happened to be on top, so I started reading it immediately after our shared appearance on *Where Did the Road Go?*

As mentioned in Chapter 5, *The Messengers* deals with owls and synchronicity, particularly in relation to the UFO and "alien abductee" phenomena. Without turning this into a book review, I will say, without reservation, that it is a book that should be on the shelf of anyone who is interested in The Other.

I wasn't an "owl person" before reading *The Messengers*, and I was determined not to become one afterward. It's not that I didn't like owls - they are incredible creatures! - It is simply that I felt that owls were kind of "Mike's thing". He literally wrote the book on them in terms of their relationship to the paranormal. What could I add to the discussion? The Other, it would seem, had different plans.

Owls had not really featured in my life previous to reading *The Messengers* - at least not significantly. In fact, I felt there was a distinct *lack* of owls in my life. I always thought there should be owls on the farm where I grew up. We had a barn, after all - where were the barn owls?! In all of my youth, however, I only saw one or perhaps two - and those were just flying across the road illuminated by car headlights. I had never gotten a good look at an owl in the wild.

The only possible strangeness I ever experienced regarding owls previous to reading *The Messengers,* was in what would be the first house Alison and I purchased. Upon our initial walk-through, the owners had owl statues and pictures everywhere. Perhaps it is significant that, while living at this house, we got married and had our twin children (via a very intense period of infertility, premature birth, and long hospital stays for both mother and babies). I was also diagnosed with Multiple Sclerosis and went on to have three rather intense experiences with The Other as well while we were living at this address (these particular experiences again fall outside the purview of this volume). A lot of very meaningful, important and challenging things happened while we were living there, but it is only with hindsight that I can assign any meaning to those owl statues being in that house on that first tour.

Around the time I was reading *The Messengers*, I was also working on my second and third books, *Bigfoot in Pennsylvania*, and *Bigfoot: West Coast Wild Men*. These books both reprint historical newspaper articles which seem to describe bigfoot sightings. As the terms "bigfoot" and "Sasquatch" were not in common usage until the late 20th century, most often these creatures are described as "wild men" in the old articles.

I was getting somewhat tired of drawing nothing but bigfoot illustrations, so I looked for something else to illustrate as well - just to add some variety to my artistic life. I settled upon Geoffrey of Monmouth's *Vita Merlini* or *The Life of Merlin*. It was something that interested me, but was very different from the bigfoot illustrations I was doing for the "wild men" books.

Upon finishing *The Messengers*, owl synchronicities began to manifest in my life. One day I walked into an antique shop only to find an entire shelf of owl figurines and small statues selling for $1.00 each. I had neither the desire nor the intention to begin collecting owls, but I was drawn to one small statue in particular. Unlike the other porcelain figurines which attempted a somewhat realistic depiction of one owl species or another, this statue was a stylized owl carved from wood, somewhat rough-hewn in a folk art style. I picked it up and turned it over in my hand. The entire back of the owl was carved into a bearded human face, framed by long hair. It looked like a typical depiction of a wizard. I immediately made the connection to Merlin and owls. I purchased this statue and brought it home with me.

Shortly afterward, I was hiking in Hex Hollow on a winding trail I didn't usually walk, making my way to the "chessboard". I was thinking, with wonder, about the owl statue with the wizard's face on its back. What are the chances that I should find it, be drawn to just that statue, and that it should be so cheap? It felt like it was waiting for me. I was suddenly struck with another realization. There is a point in Merlin's life where he retires to the woods and forsakes society. He lives as a hermit, learns to speak to animals, and is considered insane. At this stage of Merlin's life, he is often referred to as a "wild man".

I was almost staggered by the layers of synchronicity. Merlin, owls, and wild men! The owl statue with the wizard's face! I thought these must be signs that I am on the right track - whatever track that is - and that is the exact instant I heard the sound.

Something large took off from the trees to my left and flew diagonally down and across the path, disappearing into the trees on the other side.

It was a barred owl.

Asking for Antlers

One of the many stories from *The Messengers* which stuck with me, was one of a woman who could sort of summon owls. As Mike related, it seemed she would only have to say "I would like to see an owl today," and at some point during the day, she would see an owl. I am not usually prone to this sort of "New Age" thinking - the idea that if you put a thought or desire "out there" that the universe (or whoever) will grant your wish. It is interesting, but I can't help but feel it's an oversimplification; if not an outright dumbing down, of the way The Other works.

That said, I am not above experimentation. What would it hurt to try? However, I didn't want to ask for an owl. As I mentioned previously, I collect skulls and bones. So, sometime in the early spring of 2017, I arrived at Hex Hollow for my usual hike. I stated aloud that I would like to find antlers.

I was on one of my two usual routes to the chessboard when something white caught my eye. It was a few yards off the trail and blowing around in the breeze. I thought at first that it must be a white plastic bag and got angry at whoever left it hanging there.

As I approached, I was, once again, stunned by synchronicity. There, at eye level, stuck on a tiny point of a branch, was a clump of white feathers. It was the entire tail section of a barn owl! I asked for antlers but I received an owl anyway!

(It is around this time that I found the deer skull at Toad Road; and, after that, began to find skulls at so many other places of interest. Likewise, summer 2017, found a barred owl take up residence near my current home - I heard it hooting often at night - And, it was, also, when we first started hearing the screech owls at Site 7.)

Blood Offering

The "chess" game continued well into the spring of 2017. I never again felt the intense fear or smelled the sickening smells, nor did I notice any more unusual sounds. The stones, however, continued to be changed almost every time I visited.

One day as I was stacking the white quartz, I cut myself badly on one of the sharp edges of the rocks. Before I noticed the wound, I had bled on a good many of the "chess pieces". "This should really intensify things," I thought.

The opposite happened. The cairns were never moved again. The "chess game" was over, at least in that location.

Be Careful What You Ask For

Sometime in late 2017, I found another cairn in Hex Hollow, which I did not make, located well off trail. I began to, once again, change and add to the cairn. The game is different now. It is more subtle. For the most part, whatever changes I make seem to just be undone and the cairn returned to the way I found it. The changes do not happen as frequently as they did at the "chessboard" either.

Every now and then, I would leave a bit of food at this cairn - usually an apple or a bit of granola - knowing, most probably, it was taken by squirrels or raccoons - but it was another way to monitor when things changed.

I started finding stick structures in the region of the cairn. Sometimes they would appear overnight. Sticks and branches woven together - sometimes living trees were bent into these formations. They were not simple snow breaks or storm damage. Whoever - or whatever - was making these things had to have hands. I was also finding X structures, twisted trees, and other curious formations which I had not previously noticed.

Having had results, if not success, when asking for antlers, I decided one day in the spring of 2018, to ask aloud once more - this time for a skull. I went to the cairn, left a bit of food, and, in the hollow of a tree beside the cairn, a tiny corked bottle of wine. I then asked aloud for a skull. (PLEASE NOTE: I do not litter - the bottle was glass and very small and I intended to retrieve it on a future visit should it remain in the hollow)

If what I am dealing with is some kind of wight - a nature spirit, perhaps - this food and alcohol would be seen as an offering. Our ancestors did it to appease spirits of all types. The tradition continues, to this day, when we leave milk and cookies out for Santa on Christmas Eve. I reasoned that, since I was asking for something, I should leave something as well.

I went on my way, and, as I hiked through a field, my attention was drawn to a clump of trees I had never noticed before. In the middle of a field, directly between my old "chessboard" and the other cairn, was this round island of trees, perhaps ¼ of an acre in size. If this curious little wood were in Ireland, it would perhaps be called a *faerie fort* - clumps of trees often grown up around the remains of iron age dwellings or mounds, and, said to be, the home of faeries, or perhaps the entrance to faerie land.

There are no faerie forts in the United States - or so I've been told - so this curious island of trees in Hex Hollow cannot be a faerie fort. However, inside, there stands a mound of stones, surrounded by the circular wood. Perhaps it serves the same function.

I was drawn to this island, having never explored it before this day. When I entered the ring of trees, the feeling became oppressive. I forced myself to press on, toward the center mound. I started to see little clumps of fur lying all around. Looking closer, I saw the head of a groundhog. Just the head, still covered in fur, with the jaw ripped off. The body was not in sight. It was a fresh kill. I asked for, and received a skull - this one just happened to be still covered in fur and gore! I left the groundhog head and jaw where it lay, and backed out of the circle of trees.

Rock mound in the "fae fort", Hex Hollow.

The groundhog's jaw as I found it.

As I made my way away from the tree-island, I walked toward the location of my old "chessboard". It was then I realized that this circular clump of trees was about where I had heard the wood knock and clicking gear sounds on that frightening day in January of 2017.

I looked for the bottle of wine in the hollow of the tree upon my next visit. It was not there. On the visit after that, however, the wine was back in the hollow. Curious, I left it there again only to have it disappear once more. I have not seen it since.

The Goblin Raccoon

Late summer of 2018 brought with it another series of synchronicities in Hex Hollow.

On the night of September 7, I was discussing synchronicity with Clint Granberry, host of the OK Talk podcast. It was a long conversation that shifted easily from one topic to another, as my conversations with Clint frequently do. Among the many things we discussed, Clint related a bit of country folklore instructing one on the means to catch a raccoon. (It is said that if one places a shiny object in a jug – that a raccoon will grab the object, and not release it. You will find the raccoon with its arm stuck in the jug the following day.) We discussed the idea of The Other being very much like The Eye of Sauron - a metaphor we arrived at independently of each other (a synchronicity unto itself!); and we discussed Seth Breedlove, the creator of the Small Town Monsters series of documentaries. These films explore sightings of cryptid creatures and other related phenomena across the United States.

My discussion with Clint extended into the early morning of Saturday, September 8. I ended our talk, noting that I had promised to go hiking that day with my son, Gideon. After getting a few hours sleep and waking up later than I intended, Gideon and I decided to head for the closest trails to make the most of our time. Those trails are in Hex Hollow.

September 8 was rainy and wet - worth noting due to the number of paranormal events which occur during or just after rain events - but neither Gideon nor I mind hiking in the rain. I am fond of a phrase my father used, and often repeat it to my wife when she asks if I am really going to hike in the rain: *It's just water and I'm not made of sugar.*

We parked in an area which is called the Crossroads parking lot. It falls, literally, at a crossroads - those incredibly liminal zones imbued with occult power and folkloric symbolism. Witches cast powerful spells at crossroads; cunning men visited crossroads on Old Christmas Eve to divine the following year's fortunes; bluesmen met the Devil at crossroads to trade their souls for musical talent or success. Certainly volumes can be written on crossroads folklore - more than I can attend to in this text - but it is notable that this particular hike would begin and end, quite literally, at a crossroads, and from a parking area *named* Crossroads.

Most of our hike was pleasant and uneventful. We made our way on a winding path through the woods and high grasses and ended up at another crossroads. Our trail crossed the main path (what was once a passable road, but now simply serves as a trail - yet another Ghost Road) and we had a decision to make: travel back to the parking lot via the easier main path, or take the muddier, messier, circuitous route through the wilder woods.

Gideon, dependably adventurous, chose the road less taken - or the trail, in this case. The rain tapered off to a light mist. We made our way through the woods, paralleling the east branch of Codorus Creek (the Codorus winds its way through many places of paranormal interest in York County). About halfway back to the parking area, the trail splits into a Y. The right fork leads away from the parking area, so we proceeded to the left.

Gideon almost always takes the lead in our hikes. He is younger and in better shape, so rather than be held to my pace, he often walks some 20 yards ahead of me. Shortly after taking the left trail at the fork, Gideon stopped and straightened up. I caught up to him and he asked, "Is that a raccoon up there?"

It was - and quite a large raccoon at that; perhaps 20 or 30 yards down the trail. It was standing up on its hind legs and looking directly at us. Seeing a raccoon in the daytime is unusual, but that, in and of itself, is not cause for any real alarm. However, I suggested we backtrack and take another trail.

As we turned to go, the raccoon began trotting towards us. I told Gideon to run. I began to run myself but turned to look back and it became apparent that we were not going to outrun this animal.

The raccoon had accelerated to a full run, hissing, gurgling, and growling as it came. There was only one thing to do: face it down. I knew the raccoon was going to either attack me - or worse - get by me and attack Gideon. There were no other options.

I walk with a large hiking stick. It has been called, and for all intents and purposes, really *is* a wizard's staff. It is covered with inlays and wood-burnt symbols of protection and personal significance.

I had one shot. If I didn't stop the raccoon with the staff, it would be down to close quarters hand-to-hand combat. Luckily, it did not come to that.

Whether by skill, luck, or divine intervention I cannot say - but my first blow struck true. It appeared to break the animal's back. Filled with adrenaline - and fear for my son's safety - I hit it one or two more times. Even as adrenaline flooded my body, my mind was clear enough to be thinking "rabies" and I know animals cannot be tested for rabies if you destroy the brain, so I was hitting behind the head.

At this point, I tripped and fell backwards. I thought for sure I was in a bad position - not knowing the extent to which I had incapacitated the raccoon. I have Multiple Sclerosis and fall on hikes somewhat regularly. One of the reasons I carry the staff is that it helps me get up when I fall. This process, however, usually takes up to a minute. Adrenaline quickened that to seconds - I sprang to my feet. Still afraid it might pursue us, I hit the raccoon a few more times with my staff, then made my way down the trail and caught up to Gideon.

Shortly after we passed the raccoon, a woman came walking by. She had nothing with her - no walking stick. Nothing to defend herself. As we made our way back to the parking lot, we passed a family with multiple young children aging, by my estimation, from six to ten years old. If the raccoon had to come after someone on the trails that day, I'm glad it was me. I was the most prepared.

We returned to the Crossroads parking lot and called a park ranger. About 20 minutes later, he showed up. The ranger's name tag read "Breedlove".

What followed was a frustrating comedy of errors and pass-the-buck bureaucracy.

The ranger found the raccoon and brought it back in a garbage bag. I asked him if it would be tested for rabies. He said since I hadn't been bitten or scratched, their policy was simply to throw the animal in a dumpster. I replied that I would like to know if the animal had rabies due to open cuts on my legs (from thorns) - and the fact that the ranger stated the raccoon had open wounds on its head when he found it.

The ranger said that if I took the animal to the hospital they would test it for rabies. This sounded odd to me, but never having dealt with this situation, I thought the ranger knew the proper procedures. He proceeded to hand me a garbage bag with the probably-rabid corpse of a raccoon. I put it in the back of my jeep and headed for the hospital.

Medical advice was, as I thought, to get rabies shots. Due to my open wounds and the proximity of the animal, a better-safe-than-sorry policy is enacted. Rabies is not a disease one survives. The rabies vaccine requires a series of 8 shots the first day (plus an extra for tetanus), with three follow-up visits for more shots.

I knew better than to bring a bag holding a dead raccoon into the hospital, but asked about getting the animal tested. The hospital staff was shocked that the ranger had given me the animal, and, as I suspected, they wanted nothing to do with the raccoon corpse. The hospital told us to call Animal Control.

Animal Control did not want the dead raccoon. They told us to call the Game Commission. The Game Commission did not want the raccoon either. They told us to burn the body. We have neither the facilities nor the will to run a raccoon crematorium, so we called the Park Service back again to see if they would deposit the animal in whatever dumpster the ranger originally wanted to dispose of it. The Park Service refused this request, essentially telling us: you took the raccoon, it's your problem now. We were left, quite literally, holding the bag - and that bag contained the body of a dead raccoon which was most likely infected with rabies.

You would think that the powers-that-be in York County would want to know if there were rabid raccoons attacking people here. You would think that there would be definite procedures in place dictating how to deal with such situations. If there are, neither the rangers, Park Service, Animal Control, nor the Game Commission are informed of said procedures!

We buried the raccoon.

Monday morning, I received a call from a woman at the Health Department asking me the whereabouts of the raccoon corpse. I informed her that it was underground. She said that ALL animal attacks - regardless of whether a person is bitten or scratched - are to be tested for rabies. I mentioned that she might want to inform the other officials involved of said policy.

The synchronicities woven into this event didn't all hit me at once. Instead, they kind of seeped into my consciousness over the course of a few days.

Upon seeing the ranger's name tag, I did think to myself that Breedlove is not such a common name and that it was funny that Clint and I had talked about Seth Breedlove the night before.

It was Clint who reminded me that we had been talking about how to catch raccoons.

Moments after the attack, I had made the joke that my one regret was not shouting "You shall not pass!" as I brought my staff down upon the raccoon - a reference to a scene from the Lord of the Rings wherein the wizard Gandalf faces down a demon on a bridge, staff in hand.

Clint and I both remarked about the "Eye of Sauron feeling" of the whole event. It started at a literal crossroads, *named* Crossroads; on a rainy, misty day; beside the Codorus Creek; in Hex Hollow - where I had had so many other strange experiences. I was attacked by an animal we had discussed at some length. I stopped it with my wizard staff (and of course there was my previous owl / Merlin / wizard / wild man experience in Hex Hollow). The ranger who showed up was named Breedlove.

It was all a bit too much. The usual feelings of wonder in regards to synchronicty were absent. This was something far darker. It felt, instead, like being punched in the stomach. I am sure part of this feeling it is due to my son's presence in what was a dangerous situation. It seemed to go deeper than my fatherly instincts of protection, however.

The Other doesn't always give you what you want. It seems to be bent on demonstrating that it will not be controlled. It cannot be predicted. Sometimes The Other will play almost childlike innocent games. Alternately, it can manifest in very dark and frightening ways. In this, it very much embodies the Trickster archetype that so many have draped over The Other before: a mask that may represent the true face of The Other as well as any of the many masks it wears.

A long period of reflection followed the raccoon attack. My last two "wondrous strange" incidents at Hex Hollow involved a freshly decapitated groundhog and a rabid raccoon attack. Neither would fall into the "nice" category.

And yet...

For what it's worth, those protective symbols on my staff *worked*. That attack could have gone horribly wrong. A good friend's mother was attacked by a raccoon in her garden, and rabies ended up being far less of a concern than the infections from the bites she suffered. I stopped the attack - most likely with my first blow. I didn't get bitten. Gideon did not get hurt, nor did he have to get the rabies vaccine shots.

For 40 years or more, I have wandered the woods. I've never been attacked by an animal before (save for yellow jackets upon disturbing their nests). I have never thought of myself as the bravest or most capable of men; and, yet, when called upon by circumstances out of my control, I did what was necessary. I hope I never have to face anything like that raccoon attack again, but I do have confidence now that if I have to, I can and will do what needs to be done.

As a person who deals with synchronicity and symbol, I am left wondering: What was I being told? Is this just The Other randomly shuffling the cards and I simply got a bum hand dealt to me on September 8? Or was there a message behind all of this?

I expect I'll be asking these questions again and again going forward. I do have one answer - and it is the advice I would give to anyone entering into exchanges with The Other. It is advice I will try to heed myself, wherever these strange roads may take me in the future:

Proceed with caution.

END NOTES

I cannot offer any answers to the mysteries of which I write. Neither can I offer many arguments to those who will say synchronicity is simply coincidence, folklore is simply fiction, and witnesses to the unexplained, are simply mistaken (or crazy). It is not my job to convince skeptics that The Other exists - or to offer conclusive evidence of the paranormal that mainstream science will accept.

I have seen the shaking hands of grown men who have told me their accounts of witnessing bigfoot. I have heard witnesses thousands of miles apart describe the same details and behaviors of spirit entities - without knowing each other or said details beforehand. I have witnessed the wonder in people's faces as they see mystery lights. I have had my own encounters, many related in this volume, which make me either an experiencer or a crazy person, according to your belief.

The world, it seems, is haunted. The Other seems to be reaching out to us from somewhere beyond. Certain places like Toad Road and Site 7 may be especially receptive to the activity. Perhaps certain people are more receptive as well.

I will keep pulling the threads, as Mike suggested. I don't expect to find an end to them, but I will keep pulling. That *is* my job. It is an interesting one, to say the least.

AFTERWORD: Confronting The Other

by Clinton Granberry

I couldn't have been older than 12 when I was first introduced to 'gothic horror' via the 1898 classic "The Turn of The Screw". I distinctly remember the fascination with the story, now retold in various forms, of a family living on an old estate, who become convinced the grounds are most certainly "haunted". Rather than being your standard ghost story however, the 'Screw' places you inside the veil between the living and the dead, and raises the ambiguity of knowing the difference. The literary scholar Oliver Elton wrote about the Screw "There is...doubt, raised and kept hanging, whether, after all, the two ghosts who can choose to which persons they will appear, are facts, or delusions of the young governess who tells the story."

Who are we to question the ghosts? Perhaps we are the spooks disturbing their tranquility, and in doing so creating what someone would call "paranormal activity". The challenge is the implementation of the thought exercise, not in the thought itself.

This field of research and study is beset by limitations placed upon it by those engaged in a different game altogether. The same rules that apply to the study of apes in the Congo have no merit to the activities on Toad Road. Yes, extraordinary claims do require extraordinary evidence. They also require extraordinary minds to unveil them and likewise receive them.

Clinton Granberry ~ October 2018

BIBLIOGRAPHY

• *Adams County News*. "Coyle Murder Recalled". Gettysburg, Pennsylvania: Adams County News, May 21, 1910.

• Clelland, Mike. *The Messengers*. (Richard Dolan Press, 2015)

• *The Courier*. "Wild Man Reported". Harrisburg, Pennsylvania: The Courier, June 22, 1913.

• Cutchin, Joshua. *The High Strangeness of Bigfoot* from *Wood Knocks Journal of Sasquatch Research*, Volume 3. (Leprechaun Press, 2018)

       Thieves in the Night: A Brief History of Supernatural Child Abductions. (Anomalist Books, 2018)

• Dickerson, Cody. *The Language of the Corpse*. (Three Hands Press, 2016)

• *The Gazette and Daily*. "Fifty Years Ago". York, Pennsylvania: Gazette and Daily, February 13, 1939.

• *Harrisburg Daily Independent*. "See Wild Man". Harrisburg, Pennsylvania: Harrisburg Daily Independent, June 16, 1913.

• *The Hazleton Sentinel*. "Blown to Pieces". Hazleton, Pennsylvania: Hazleton Sentinel, February 14, 1889.

• Paulides, David. *Missing 411: The Devil's in the Details*. (CreateSpace Independent Publishing Platform, 2014)

• *Pittsburgh Dispatch*. "Three Albinos in One Family". Pittsburgh, Pennsylvania: Pittsburgh Dispatch, May 16, 1889.

• Renner, Timothy. *Beyond the Seventh Gate*. (CreateSpace Independent Publishing Platform, 2016)

       Bigfoot in Pennsylvania. (CreateSpace Independent Publishing Platform, 2017)

       The Company They Keep from *Wood Knocks Journal of Sasquatch Research*, Volume 3. (Leprechaun Press, 2018)

• Shoemaker, Henry W. *Pennsylvania Mountain Stories*. (Bradford Record Publishing Company, 1907)

• *Treasured Recipes.* Friends of the Welsh Cottages. (The Old Line Museum, 2008)

• *The Wilkes-Barre Record.* "Fish Walks Like a Man". Wilkes-Barre, Pennsylvania: Wilkes-Barre Record, October 23, 1905.

• *Wilkes-Barre Times Leader*. "Johnson's Dynamite Factory...". Wilkes-Barre, Pennsylvania: Wilkes-Barre Times Leader, February 15, 1889.

• Wolf, George A. and Sons. *Wolf's: Mount Wolf PA*. (George A. Wolf and Sons, undated pamphlet - possibly 1920s)

• *The York Daily*. "Searching For Treasures". York, Pennsylvania: York Daily, December 16, 1892.

       "York Naturalist Talks of Snakes". York, Pennsylvania: York Daily, April 6, 1905.

       "Case of Spooks". York, Pennsylvania: York Daily, September 26, 1905.

       "Wild Man at Accomac". York, Pennsylvania: York Daily, June 17, 1913.

       "25 Years Ago". York, Pennsylvania: York Daily, February 14, 1914.

Websites:

• Phantoms and Monsters (phantomsandmonsters.com)

• Wikipedia (en.wikipedia.org/wiki/Werehyena)

Podcasts:

• Sasquatch Chronicles. Episode 430: Strange East Texas Encounters. (www.SasquatchChronicles.com)

• Strange Familiars. Episode 19: Site 7 - An Introduction (www.StrangeFamiliars.com)

Looking across the Codorus Creek from Toad Road.

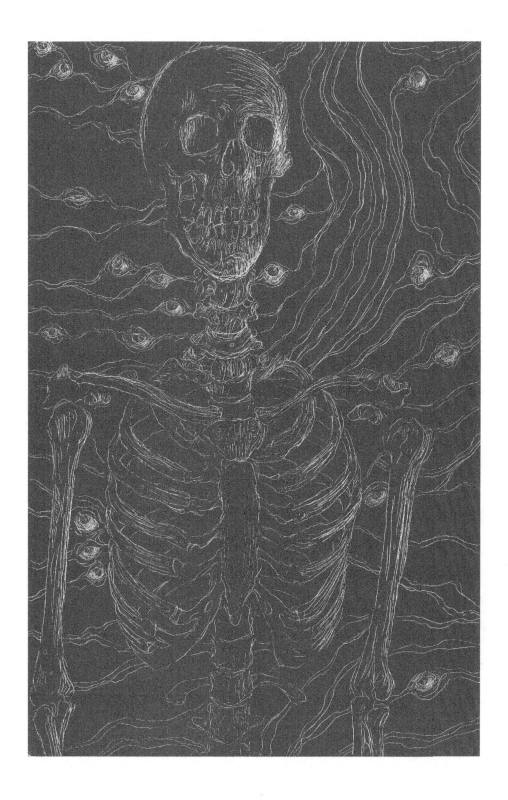

ABOUT THE AUTHOR

Timothy Renner is an author, illustrator, and folk musician living in Pennsylvania. His illustrations have appeared in the pages of various books, magazines, fanzines and comics as well as on many record and CD covers. Since 1995, Timothy has been making music both solo and with his band, Stone Breath. Timothy is the creator of *Strange Familiars*, a podcast concerning the paranormal, weird history, folklore, and the occult. He makes regular appearances on the paranormal radio show, *Where Did the Road Go?*, and has appeared as a guest on many other podcasts and radio programs, including *Coast to Coast AM*.

Other Books by Timothy:
Beyond the Seventh Gate, 2016
Bigfoot in Pennsylvania, 2017
Bigfoot: West Coast Wild Men, 2018

Photo of the author by Alison Renner.

Strange Familiars podcast explores topics ranging from cryptids, ghosts, and UFOs, to folklore, weird and forgotten history, and the occult.

If you have experienced something strange - or if you know of a story you think we should cover please contact us:

StrangeFamiliarsPodcast@gmail.com
www.StrangeFamiliars.com

Find us on iTunes, Stitcher, YouTube, or wherever you listen to podcasts.